Forex Strategy ST Patterns Trading

EUR/USD Chart An
Step by Step
300% for One Month

Vladimir Poltoratskiy

Copyright 2017-2020 by Vladimir Poltoratskiy

License Notes

This e-book is licensed for your personal enjoyment only. This e-book may not be re-sold or given away to other people. If you would like to share this book with another person, please purchase an additional copy for each recipient. If you're reading this book and did not purchase it, or it was not purchased for your use only, then please return to your favorite e-book retailer and purchase your own copy. Thank you for respecting the hard work of this author.

Risk Warning

Carrying out trading operations on the financial markets with marginal financial instruments has a high level of risk and may lead to the loss of invested funds. Before you start trading, please take all conceivable precautions and ensure that you fully recognize all risks and have all relevant knowledge for each trade. None of the trading recommendations provided in this book should be considered a provision of individual consultation for concrete investment decisions. The given recommendations can be used only as an illustration of the described principles. The author is not liable for any profits or losses that may be caused directly or indirectly by using the information presented in this book. The author describes the rules of trade that he has learned from his personal, long-term experience on the currency market. These may not necessarily reflect the views of other experts in this field who have used other trading strategies.

Table of Contents

From the Author 3
The Fundamentals of the Trading System..4
Graphic Tools..6
Trading System Parameters 7
ST Pattern Schemes...13
Analysis of the EUR/USD Currency Pair 21
Analysis of the GBP/USD Currency Pair...41
EUR/USD, M5 47
Conclusion...50
Contact...52

From the Author

My first book, *Trading Code is Open: ST Patterns of the Forex and Futures Exchanges*, was published in late April 2017. Over the following month, I received dozens of reviews via e-mail, many of them from traders thanking me for publishing the strategy and, often, asking additional questions.

Over several years, using and improving the ST Patterns trading system, I developed the ability to use the system to rapidly produce a technical analysis of stock charts. However, what now seems simple to me is often difficult for those who are studying this strategy for the first time.

About a month after the release of the first book, I realized that it was necessary to write a manual that provided step-by-step, detailed explanations of the technical part of the ST Patterns Strategy.

The demonstration of the successful operation of the technical system presented in this book is not meant to encourage readers to trade on the exchanges. The profession of a trader is one of the most difficult specialties. The purpose of this manual is to show the method of graphical analysis with which I have actually worked, which, nonetheless, cannot guarantee the receipt of real profits.

For more information about the ST Patterns Strategy you can visit my website at https://stpatterns.com: indicators, videos, daily trading strategy, answers to questions...

The Fundamentals of the Trading System

The theoretical rationale for this strategy is described in sufficient detail in the first book, but it will be briefly repeated in this manual: all the charts of liquid exchange instruments mainly consist of Structural Target Patterns or ST Patterns models. Opened models, followed one after another, create a market picture. The ability to recognize patterns and act correctly when they appear gives the trader an effective tool for technical analysis.

Levels of price peaks and recessions

If the prices of the peaks and valleys (fractal levels) are broken by a sufficient amount equal to x pips, traders push the price in the direction of the breakthrough, as shown in Figure 1.

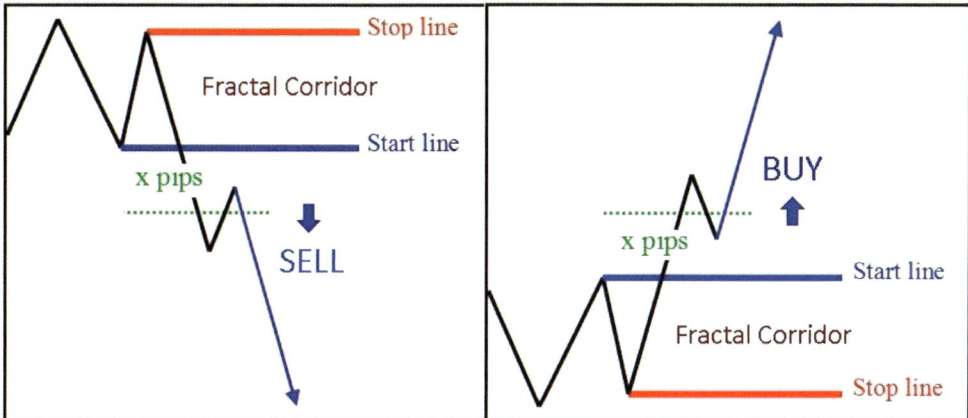

Figure 1: Breakthrough of the fractal level by x amount

To determine the local price minimum and maximum, a fractal indicator is used, which denotes local extremes using arrows. The breakthrough value of x is a variable value and can be different for each trading instrument depending on its technical characteristics, such as volatility. Additionally, this value can vary over time for the same instrument.

Fractal Corridor

At the moment of the break between the two last oppositely directed fractals, a Fractal Corridor is formed, as shown in Figures 1 and 2. The level of the Start Line coincides with the price of the broken fractal. The Stop Line corresponds to the level of the last oppositely directed fractal.

Three candle fractals

This situation is important for short-term trading. Fractal levels occur at the peaks and valleys of three candlestick fractals, which include inner side candles. An example is shown in Figure 2.

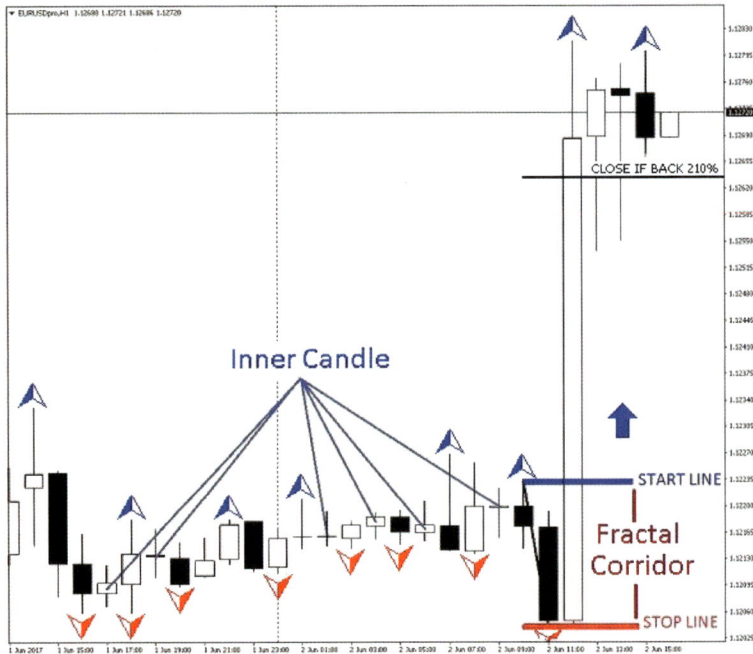

Figure 2: Breakthrough of three candle fractals with an inner candle

On the chart, there is a fractal indicator showing the upper and lower levels of the central candles in groups consisting of three candles. The condition for the appearance of the ST Pattern fractal is the presence of one candle to the left and one candle to the right of the central candle. An upper or upward fractal is formed when the high price of the central candle is equal to or greater than the high prices of the candles to its left and right. A lower or downward fractal is formed when the low price of the central candle is equal to or lower than the low prices of the candles to its left and right.

Graphic Tools

To analyze the charts, you will need three tools: a price level indicator, a fractal indicator, and an ADR (Average Daily Range) indicator.

On the top toolbar of the MetaTrader 4 software, there is an indicator for Fibonacci levels, which can be configured as shown in Figure 3 below.

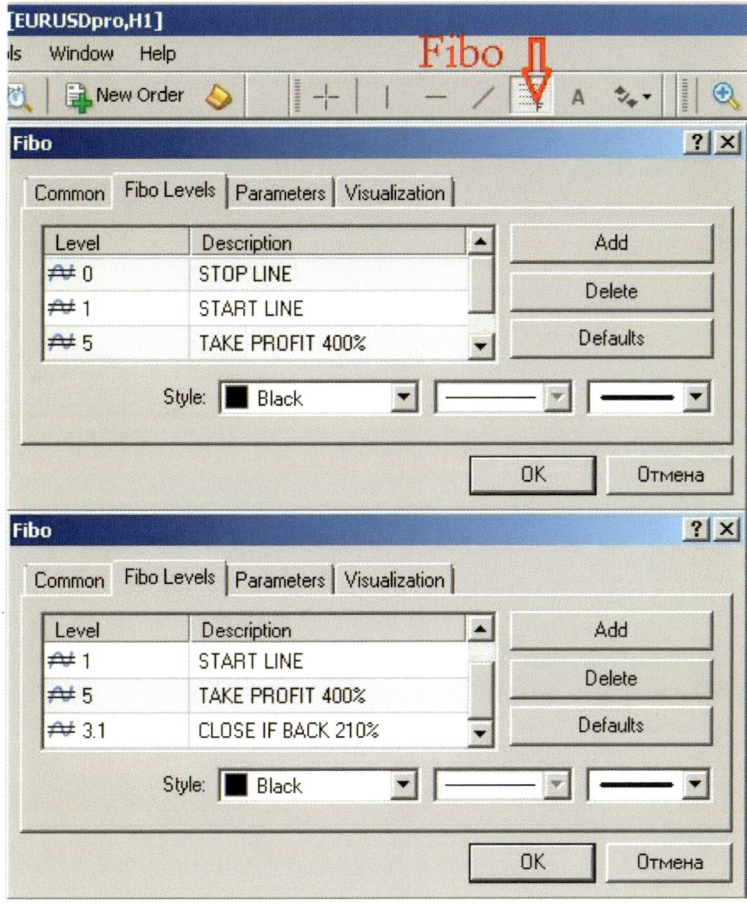

Figure 3: Trading level values

Set up this way, the Take Profit will be 400% of the height of the Fractal Corridor. The height of the Fractal Corridor itself will be equal to 100%. The level of 210% is important because in this area there can be significant price reversals in the opposite direction.

The fractal indicator and the ADR (Average Daily Range) indicator can be found independently and installed in the MT4 or MT5 trading terminals, or downloaded at: https://stpatterns.com/indicators-parameters/.

Trading System Parameters

After breaking the fractal level by the specified value (the breakout), you need to open the position in the direction of the breakout and simultaneously set the Stop Loss order and Take Profit Order. In the examples given in this manual, a value of 7 pips will be considered sufficient for breaking fractal levels of the EUR/USD pair (a more accurate value of this parameter, equal to 7.6 pips, is used in the third book, "Trading Strategy ...").

Buy Limit and Sell Limit Orders

In the *Trading Code is Open* book, the opening of the transaction occurred immediately when the price passed the start line level by 7 pips. However, this method can lead, as noted, to unwanted slippage of the price at the time of the breakthrough.

In order to avoid unnecessary losses, let's make a little change to how we enter the market when the fractal level is sufficiently broken. It is better to place pending orders once the price passes the breakout level, assuming the price will roll back slightly and allow the orders to open. The purchase order (Buy Limit Order) will be set to the Start Line level plus 7 pips, and the Sell Limit Order will be set to the Start Line level minus 6 pips. This is assuming that the chart is drawn using the bid price with a spread equal to 1 pip.

Take Profit Order

The Target or Take Profit Order should be at a distance from the level of the broken fractal or Start Line that is about four times larger than the height of the broken Fractal Corridor. In other words, the planned average profit if the Target is achieved should be approximately three times more than the possible loss, as shown in Figure 4.

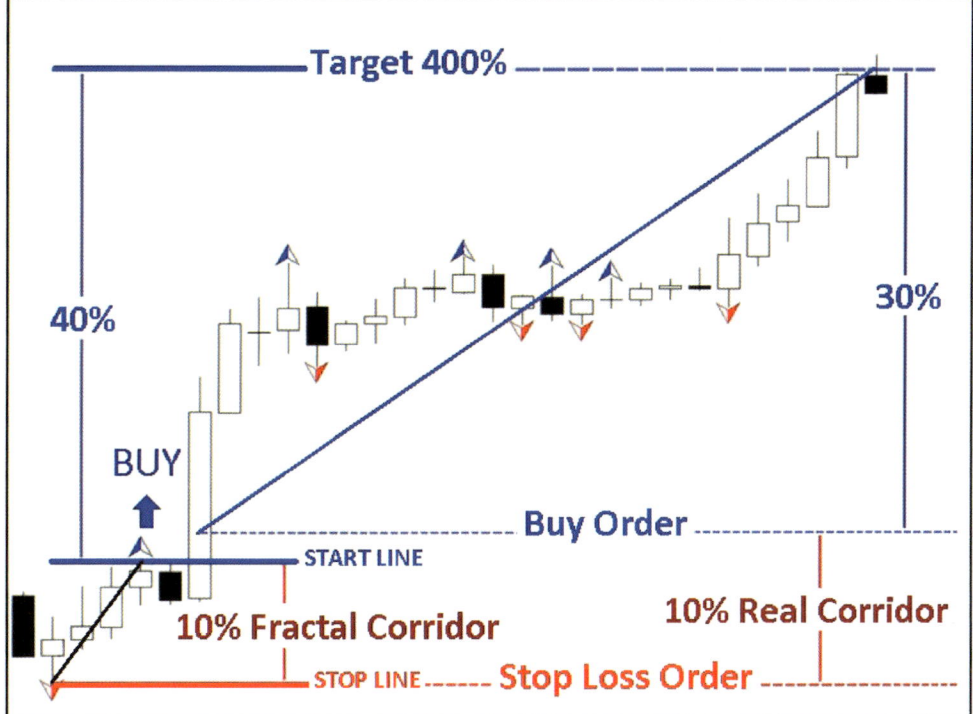

Figure 4: Profit-Loss ratio

This situation arises because, due to the breakout level, the distance between the opening level of the transaction and the Stop Loss Order is greater than the value height of the Fractal Corridor. When the price reaches the Target or Take Profit level, the trade will be closed at exactly 400% for the Buy Order and 400% plus 1 pip for the Sell Order (again assuming a spread of 1 pip). At the time of purchase, the Stop Loss Order will be located exactly at the level of the Stop Line, and when selling, it will be located 1 pip higher than the Stop Line level.

With such variable values and a Fractal Corridor height of about 26 pips, the profit will be at the Target level of 400% of the height of the Fractal Corridor, which is three times greater than the loss. A Fractal Corridor with a height of less than 26 pips in height will produce a smaller result, and one with a height of more than 26 pips will produce a higher one.

Start Line and Stop Line

The Start Line always coincides with the level of a fully formed three candlestick fractal that was fractured by a sufficient amount. The location of the Stop Line depends on the direction of the previous movement, i.e., the direction of the previous ST Pattern's movement.

It is important to determine the Stop Line correctly, because the Stop Loss Order will be placed near its level. The logic of how to determine the stop line can seem more complicated than it actually is. When the price reverses direction, there is inertia from the previous direction that must be taken into account to find the most reliable level for the Stop Line. When continuing the price movement in the same direction, the requirements for installing the Stop Line are less strict.

Traders who know the difference in the game for and against the trend must understand the need for different approaches to installing the Stop Loss Order depending on the direction of the trend.

For a better understanding of the rules for installing the Stop Line, you need to understand the definitions of "fully formed" fractal and "not fully formed" (aka partially formed) fractal. The difference between these is shown in Figure 5.

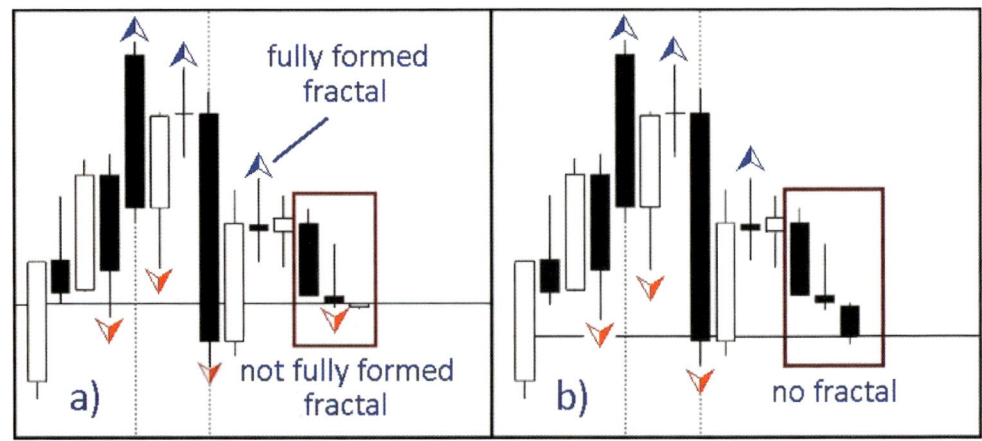

Figure 5: Fully formed fractal and not fully formed fractal

All fractals in Figure 5a are fully formed fractals, with the exception of the last one. The last fractal has only two completed candles, as the third candle is not yet fully closed. Such a fractal with two closed and one incomplete candle can be called a "not fully formed fractal." Figure 5b shows that the last not fully formed fractal was canceled after the breakdown at the price of the fractal level. A fully formed fractal cannot be canceled.

All the graphic combinations shown below have the same Stop Line installation rules for similar models that are flipped horizontally in the other direction.

Figure 6 shows the situation in which a new Fractal Corridor is formed in the direction of the previous movement.

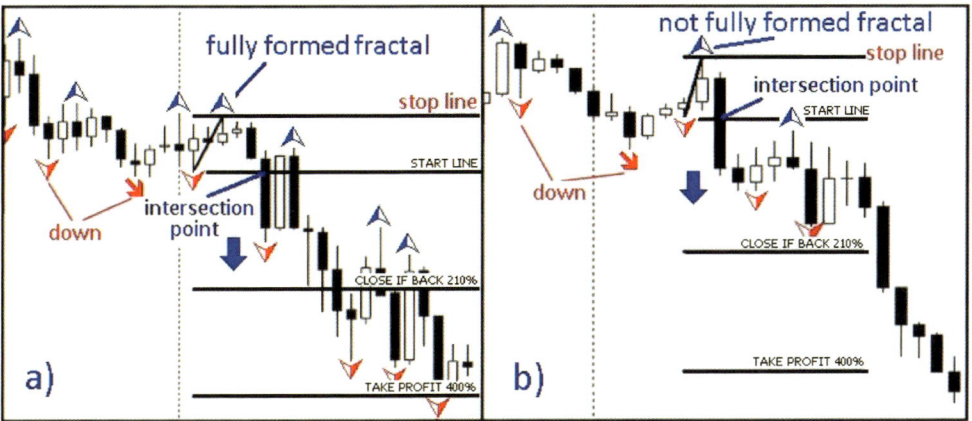

Figure 6: Placement of the Stop Line when the traffic continues

A new Fractal Corridor is formed when the price crosses the fractal level.

When a new Fractal Corridor is formed in the same direction as the previous movement, the Stop Line is located at the level of the opposite fully formed or partially formed fractal that is closest to the point of intersection of the Starting Line.

The rules for placing the Stop Line when reversing the direction of the previous movement are shown in Figure 7.

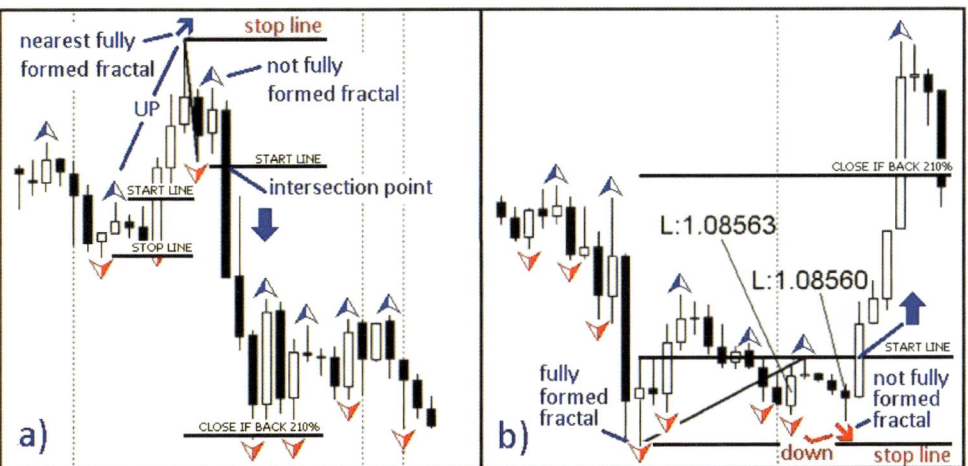

Figure 7: Stop Line at the level of a fully formed fractal when the price reverses

When a new Fractal Corridor is formed in the opposite direction of the previous movement, the Stop Line is placed only at the level of the opposite fully formed fractal that is closest to the point of intersection of the Starting Line. Partially formed fractals are not used in this case.

a) The Stop Line is placed only at the level of the completely formed, nearest to the intersection of the Starting Line, opposite fractal, which is in the area of the turn. If there is no suitable opposite fractal between the Start Line fractal and the point of intersection, the nearest opposite fully formed fractal to place the Stop Line should be selected by searching backwards from the Start Line candle for a maximum of the last two days. This time period on hourly charts is referred to as the "turn area" or the "reversal zone". The level of this fractal must exceed the greatest price level between the Start Line candle and the intersection point.

For example, forming a corridor downward, the high point of this fully formed fractal should be higher than the highest point that is between the intersected fractal and the intersection point of the Start Line.

b) Accordingly, when forming a corridor upward, the low point of this fractal should be lower than the lowest point between the intersected fractal and the intersection point.

As noted, the reversal zone includes fractals that appeared on the current day and the previous one. This definition will be discussed again in the example of the ST Complex Reverse Movement Pattern, which appeared on April 25 with Corridor № 3 at the base (Figure 20).

Situations when there are no formed fractals in the reversal area are shown in Figure 8.

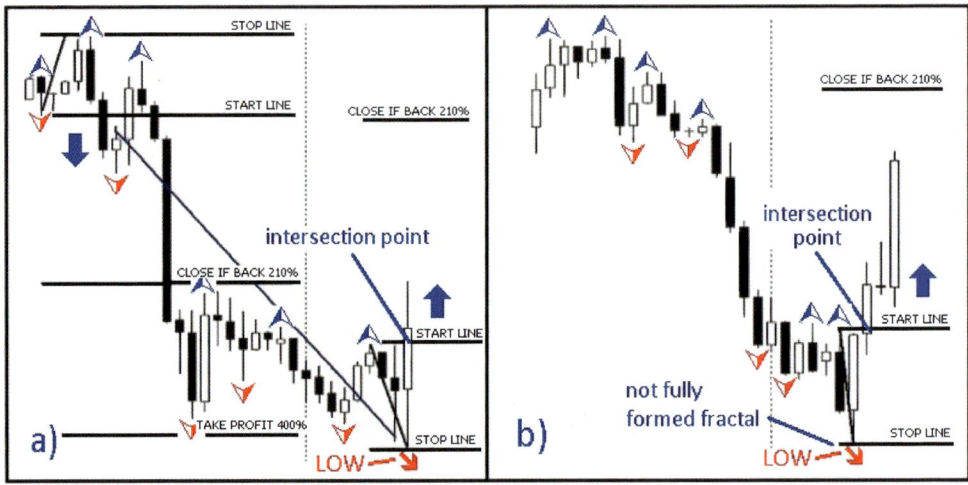

Figure 8: The absence of a fractal in the reversal zone

a) If a suitable Stop Line fractal was not found between the Start Line fractal and the intersection point, and there is also no opposite fully formed fractal in the reversal zone (whose fractal level exceeds the greatest point between the intersected fractal and the intersection point of the Start Line), the Stop Line should be positioned at the greatest point between the intersected fractal and the place of the intersection itself. In the example above, when forming a corridor upward, the greatest point is the lowest price level between the Start Line fractal and the intersection point.

b) In this case, this lowest point coincides with the level of the downward fractal that is not fully formed at the moment of intersection.

Large and Small Corridors

For more desirable results, do not use corridors which are too Large or too Small in trading. The upper permissible value of the height of the Fractal Corridor is limited to half of the value of the ADR indicator (average daily volatility for the previous completed five days).

Fractal Corridors of less than 12 pips are also better to skip because, when working with such Small Corridors, the profit decreases and the ratio of profit to loss makes the risk too high.

The estimated loss will be 10% of the deposit. This is a high percentage of loss and you should only use this value after achieving positive trading results using lower loss rates!

The *Trading Code is Open* book described about twenty ST Patterns. To analyze the EUR/USD chart from April 21 to May 31, we only need half of them. The new ST False Stairs Pattern will also be shown.

Below are diagrams and descriptions of ten ST Patterns that will be used for the analysis. All the patterns shown have their symmetrical "twin" 180 degrees from the horizontal axis.

ST Pattern Schemes

Starting ST Patterns

Starting ST Patterns appear between the time when the price overcomes the Start Line boundary and the time when the fractal level is passed by a sufficient value to create a breakout.

Two possible variants of the ST False Movement Pattern formation are shown in Figure 9.

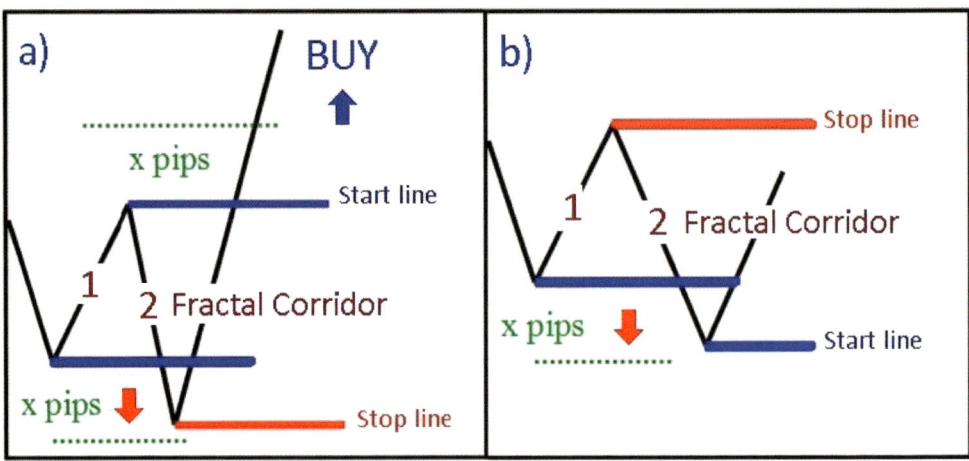

Figure 9: ST False Movement Pattern

When this pattern is formed, the price falls below the fractal level, but it cannot overcome it by a sufficient amount of x pips to fix the breakdown. Then, a new, lower fractal is formed and a new Stop Line or Start Line is placed at its level. Thus, the initial motion, which could not break through the fractal by the amount of x pips, turned out to be false.

Turning upward, the price can break through the opposite upper fractal, as shown in Figure 5a, or it can stay inside the new Corridor, as shown in Figure 5b. The ST False Movement Pattern is considered to be completely formed as soon as the new fully formed lower fractal appears.

The variable x for the EUR/USD pair in this strategy is accepted as it was written above—equal to 7 pips; going forward, the patterns' illustrations will show this value.

The ST Stairs Pattern, which is the next model that is needed for technical analysis, is shown in Figure 10.

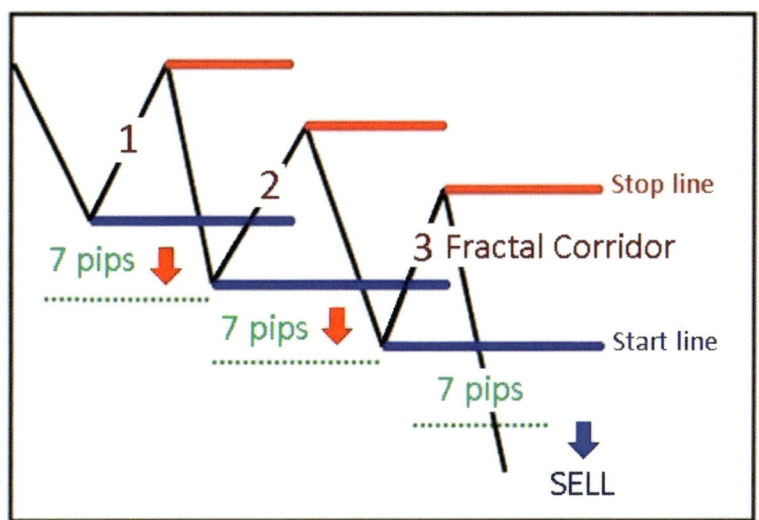

Figure 10: ST Stairs Pattern

This pattern begins with the appearance of the ST False Movement Pattern. In the process of formation, this model can create several new Fractal Corridors, and it ends when the price breaks the level of the last fully formed three candlestick fractals by 7 pips. In this situation, the position is opened downward, and the Stop Order is set near the Stop Line coinciding with the level of the last opposite fractal.

Sometimes there is a situation when the price and cannot break through the bottom fractal, and then there is a breakdown of the opposite upper fractal. Under such conditions, a new model appears, which is the ST False Stairs Pattern shown in Figure 11.

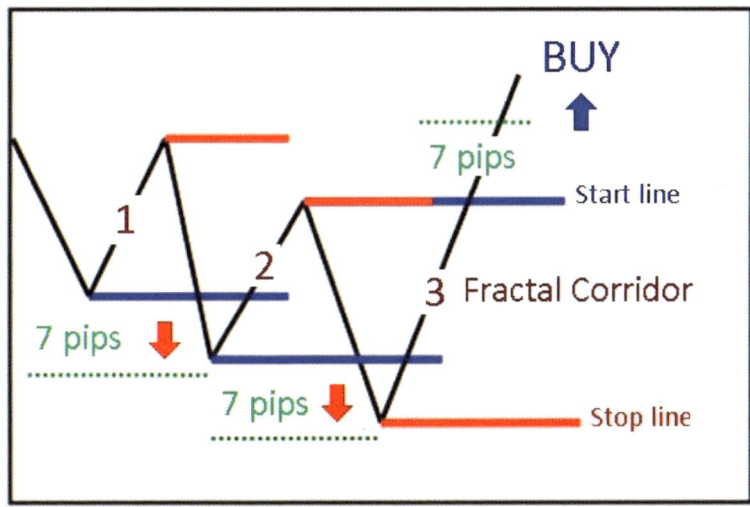

Figure 11: ST False Stairs Pattern

All ST Patterns are formed on the hourly charts, and the trader usually has enough time to recognize the reversal combinations and open the position in the desired direction.

Initial ST Patterns

Initial ST Patterns appear at a time when the price overcomes the fractal level by a sufficient amount to fix the breakdown, and they exist until the price reaches 210% of the height of the Fractal Corridor.

Periodically, there are situations in the market when the price breaks through the fractal level, and then, having developed a corridor, it can reverse direction and overcome the level of an opposite fractured fractal. In this case, the ST Reverse Movement Pattern shown in Figure 12 is formed.

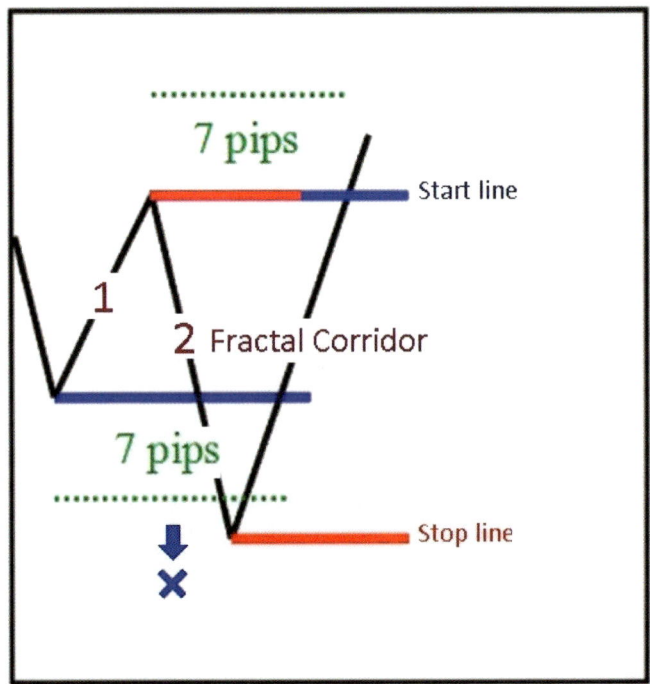

Figure 12: ST Reverse Movement Pattern

Unlike the ST False Movement Pattern, in this situation, the trader takes a loss equal to a predetermined percentage of his deposit. The model is completed when the price reaches the level of the initial Stop Loss Order.

The next ST Double Reverse Movement Pattern shown in Figure 13 can cause a loss twice in a row.

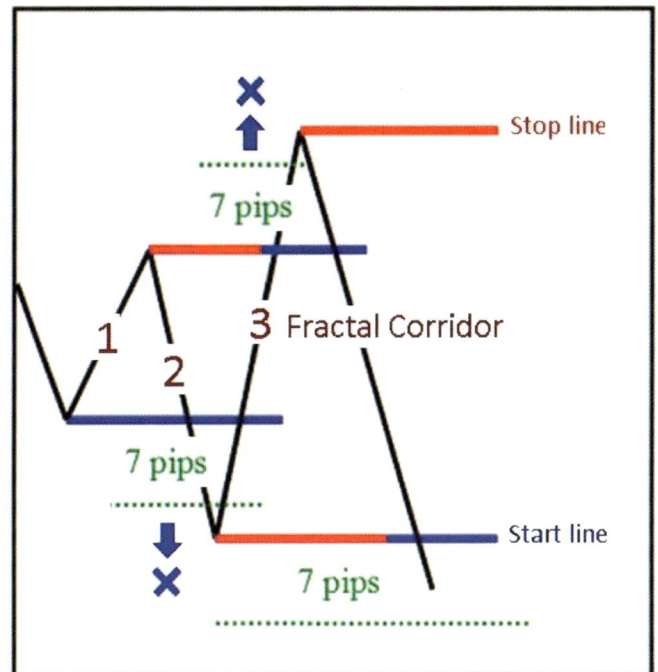

Figure 13: ST Double Reverse Movement Pattern

This model repeats the previous pattern two times in succession and ends when the second Stop Loss Order is triggered.

The ST Complex Reverse Movement Pattern is shown in Figure 14.

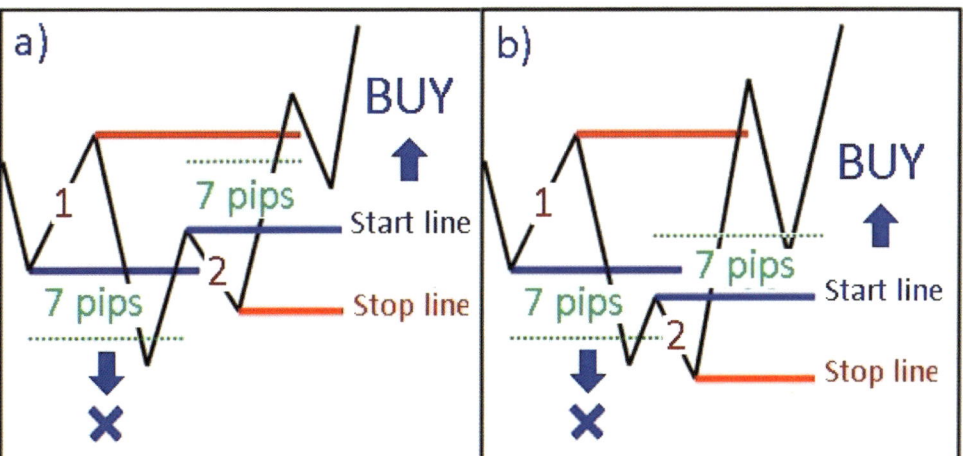

Figure 14: ST Complex Reverse Movement Pattern

a) When moving upward, the price can form one or several additional Fractal Corridors before it overcomes the Stop Line at the first Corridor. In this situation, to open a position, you should use the last Corridor that appeared before the closing of the initial position on the Stop Loss Order.

b) This concept is shown when Corridor № 2 is formed outside Corridor № 1.

The ST Double Complex Reverse Movement Pattern, which is shown in Figure 15, is more complicated.

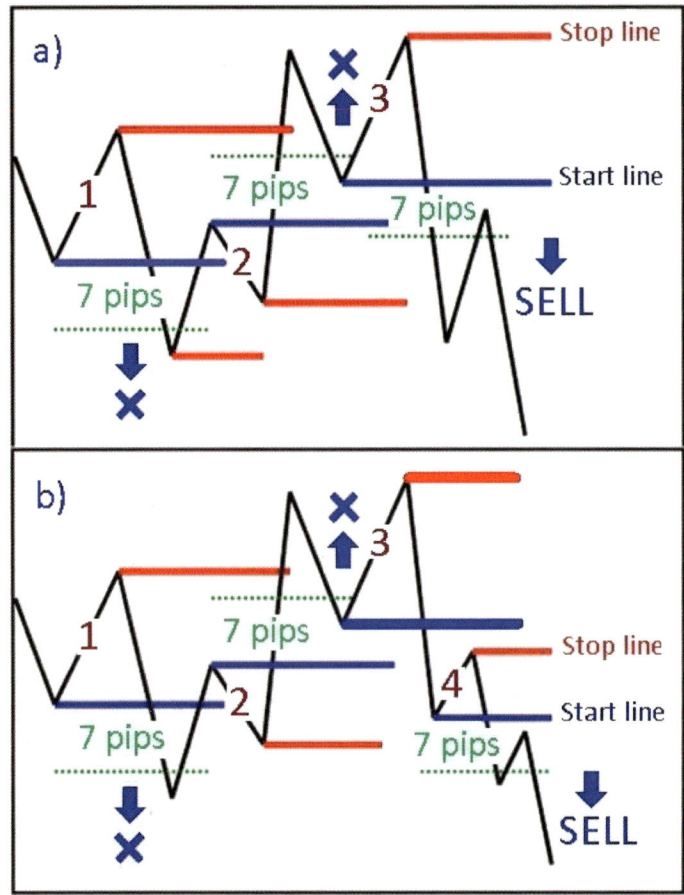

Figure 15: ST Double Complex Reverse Movement Pattern

a) The price changes its direction twice, creating additional Fractal Corridors. The model can bring a double loss before the price goes in the original direction.

b) Corridor № 3 was left out of the game because Corridor № 4 was the most recent corridor to form before the break of the Stop Line of Corridor № 2. In this case, however, the 210% and 400% levels from the height of Corridor № 3 should be taken into account.

Completion ST Patterns

Completion ST Patterns appear when the price reaches the level of 210% of the height of the Fractal Corridor and ends when the price reaches the 400% Target.

The most common completion pattern is the ST Direct Movement Pattern shown in Figure 16.

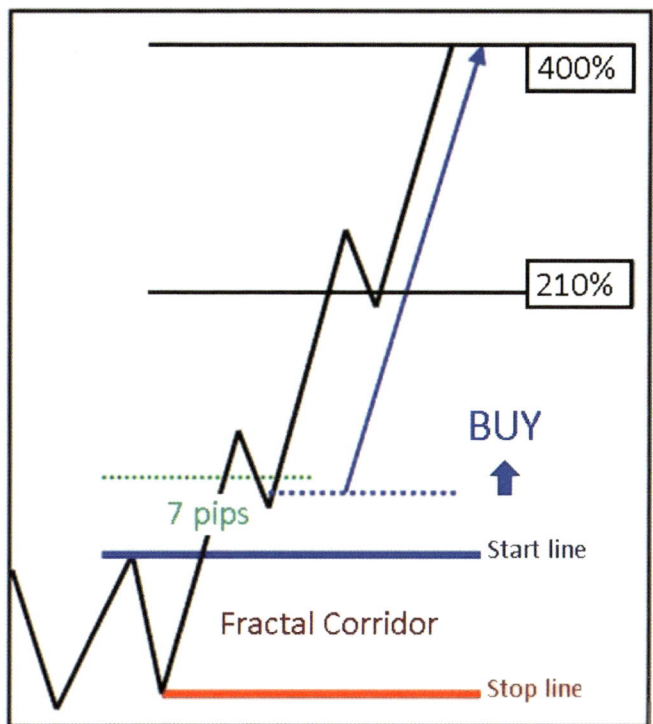

Figure 16: ST Direct Movement Pattern

This simple, profitable model can occur both on its own as well as part of other more complex Completion models. Often, this pattern completes the action of other models. When forming an ST Direct Movement Pattern, the price breaks the fractal level by 7 pips and then reaches the Target level of 400%.

Near the level of 210% of the height of the Fractal Corridor, market reversals are possible in the opposite of the original direction. At this distance from the height of the Corridor, some traders start to close their positions, fixing profits. The 2:1 ratio of the target to the height of a Fractal Corridor allows them to stay in the game, so this group of players manages to turn prices in their direction.

When quotes reach the level of 210% of the height of the Fractal Corridor, you should rearrange the Stop Loss Order to the level of the opening position (breakeven), and if the fractal breaks in the opposite direction, you must close the starting position and open a new one in the direction of the breakout.

This tactic as a whole is effective. However, periodically, a breakout that is opposite to the initial movement does not continue. Such a situation occurs in the ST Interrupted Direct Movement Pattern, which is shown in Figure 17.

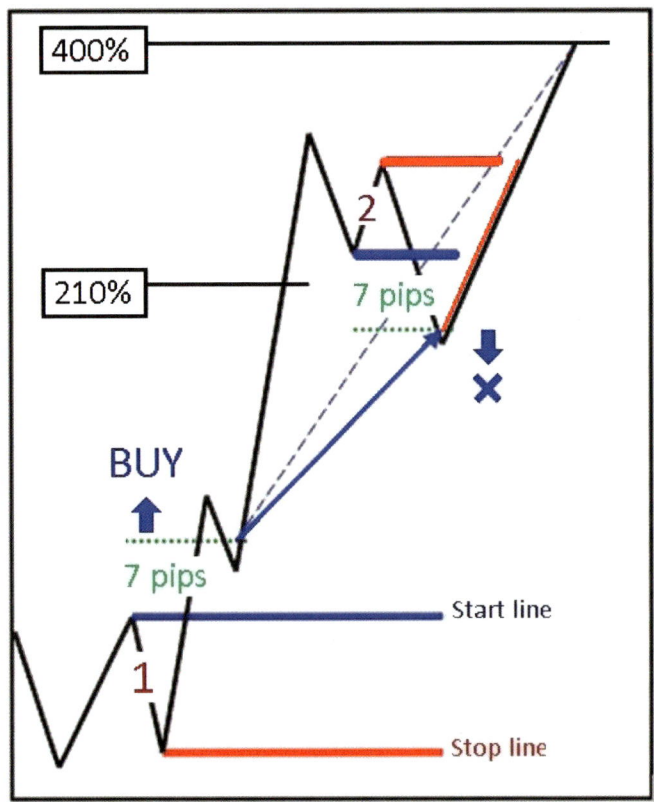

Figure 17: ST Interrupted Direct Movement Pattern

After the formation of this graphical combination, you should wait outside the market until the price reaches the original Target of 400%, or takes another attempt to move down. Other tactics are also possible while working with this model. For example, you can open a counter position without closing the original one. This so-called "Lock" technique can be effective, but these examples will not be shown. In practice, an individual trader can choose the most suitable option for this model.

A more complex and profitable ST Counter Movement with Direct Movement Pattern is shown in Figure 18.

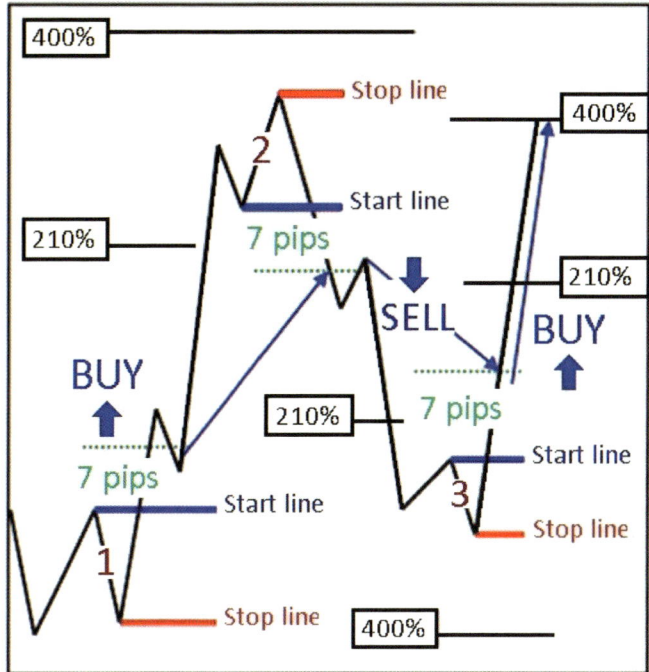

Figure 18: ST Counter Movement with Direct Movement Pattern

In the formation of this model, the price overcomes the level of 210% and then changes its direction downward. The downward movement also overcomes the level of 210% of the height of the Fractal Corridor № 2. Then, a new reversal takes place in the original upward direction, and the ST Direct Movement Pattern completes this complex pattern, which reaches the target of 400% of the height of Corridor № 3. To work with this model, you need to open positions three times, each time fixing profits from the previous deal.

The remaining ST Patterns do not appear in the following EUR/USD charts. Their descriptions, and the rules for working with them can be found in the *Trading Code is Open* book.

Analysis of the EUR/USD Currency Pair

Now that all the patterns that will be required for the analysis of the EUR/USD pair have been explained, we will conduct a step-by-step analysis of this pair's schedule from April 21 to May 31, 2017.

We set the Stop Line depending on the previous price direction. The previous direction is determined to be upward if, working backwards from the intersection point, the most recent fractal is an upward fractal that is higher than the one before it. Conversely, the previous direction is downward if, the nearest fractal to the intersection point is a downward fractal that is lower than the one before it . For more convenient visualization of the market direction on the charts, the Fractals Direction ST Patterns indicator will be used, which uses special arrows to indicate this direction. This indicator is available for download at: https://stpatterns.com/indicators-parameters/.

All the pictures shown here can be viewed more closely on your own historical charts or by downloading the images from Google Drive at: https://drive.google.com/drive/folders/0B3brjTjlH1PIVjF1cHQtbkRodFU?usp=sharing

The method for finding the beginning point of the ST Patterns is shown in Figure 19.

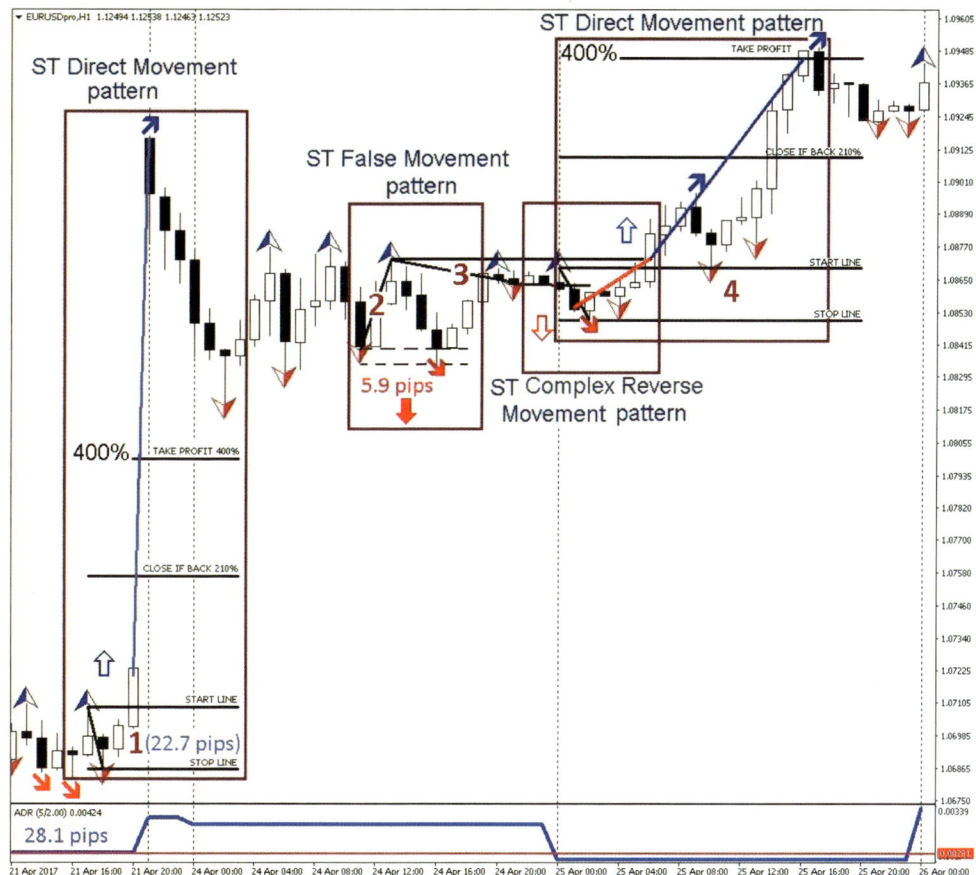

Figure 19: EUR/USD from April 21-25, 2017

In order to test the EUR/USD pair for the month of May, you need to find a place in the history of the chart where the previous ST Pattern was clearly completed. This must be done so that the internal structure of a complex pattern is not confused with an independent model.

On April 23, there was a price gap at the opening of the market after the Presidential elections in France. At this point, a self-completed ST Direct Movement Pattern with Corridor № 1 at the base was formed. From this place, we will move on, briefly analyzing the subsequent combinations until the beginning of May.

On April 24, prices were mostly flat, and overcame the lower fractal by only 5.9 pips, having formed a ST False Movement Pattern with Corridor № 2 at the bottom. A breakdown of the fractal did not take place.

In the future, I will not show all the failed breakdowns on the charts in order to not overcomplicate them. Instead, I will note only instances where the price almost reached the level of the breakthrough.

At the end of the day, a Small Corridor № 3 was formed with a height of 9.7 pips. Under the terms of the trading system, such Small Corridors should be skipped. As an exception, let's look at the example of how this ST Complex Reverse Pattern was formed, because in the future this model will no longer appear on the charts. Also, in this example, you can see how to correctly place the Stop Line.

The ST Complex Reverse Movement Pattern is shown in Figure 20.

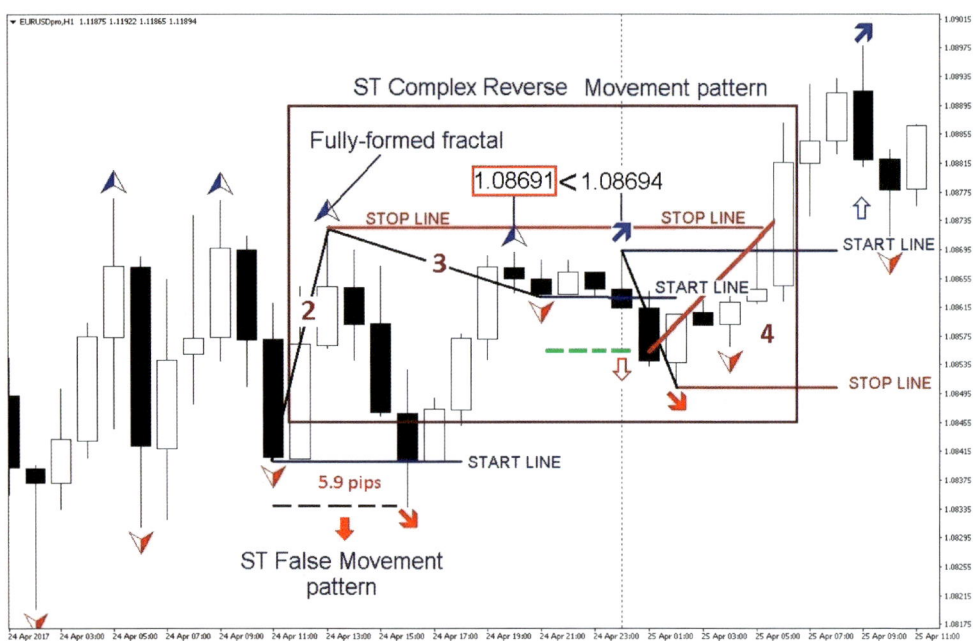

Figure 20: ST Complex Reverse Movement Pattern

At the beginning of the trading day on April 25, Corridor № 3 broke down. The direction of the previous ST False Movement Pattern was down. According to the rules of the system, the Stop Line at Corridor № 3 should be located at the level of the nearest fractal, which is opposite to the point of intersection of the Starting Line.

Between the punched fractal and the intersection point with the Start Line price there is only an unformed fractal at the time of intersection. Therefore, you need to search the history of the past two days (the reversal zone). The price of the peak of the last fractal formed before the breakdown is 1.08691. This value is less than the value of the highest peak between the intersected fractal and the intersection of the Start Line. This means that this fractal is not suitable for installing a Stop Line for Corridor № 3.

The high point of the next fractal on the left is higher than the highest point between the intersected fractal and the place where the price crosses the Start

Line at Corridor № 3. This fractal corresponds to the conditions for placing it at its Stop Line level. In this situation, the level of the Stop Line of Corridor № 3 happens to coincide with the Stop Line for Corridor № 2.

Further, the price, turning upward, overcomes the Stop Line of Corridor № 3, creating, before that, a fractal that was punched inside Corridor № 3. The level of this last fractal before the Stop Line break should be used to open the position upward. The Stop Line of Corridor № 4 is located at the level of the last fully formed opposite fractal, since the previous movement was directed downward.

On the same day, the ST Direct Movement Pattern reached the Target of 400%. Obviously, this model is also an independent and complete pattern.

Figure 21 shows a graph on which, from April 26 to May 4, a long ST Counter Movement with Direct Movement Pattern was formed. The pattern consists of several internal models and is completed when the internal ST Direct Movement Pattern reaches the Target of 400%.

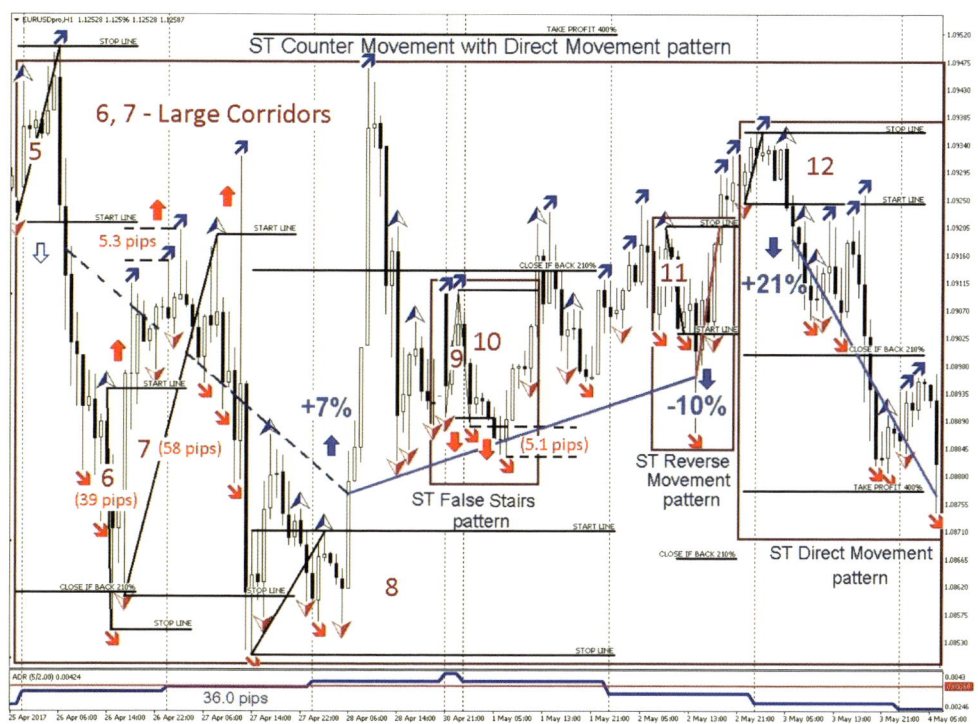

Figure 21: EUR/USD for the period from April 26 to May 4, 2017

To show the whole of the pattern, the image size had to be reduced. The following Figure 22 shows the period from April 26-28 in more detail.

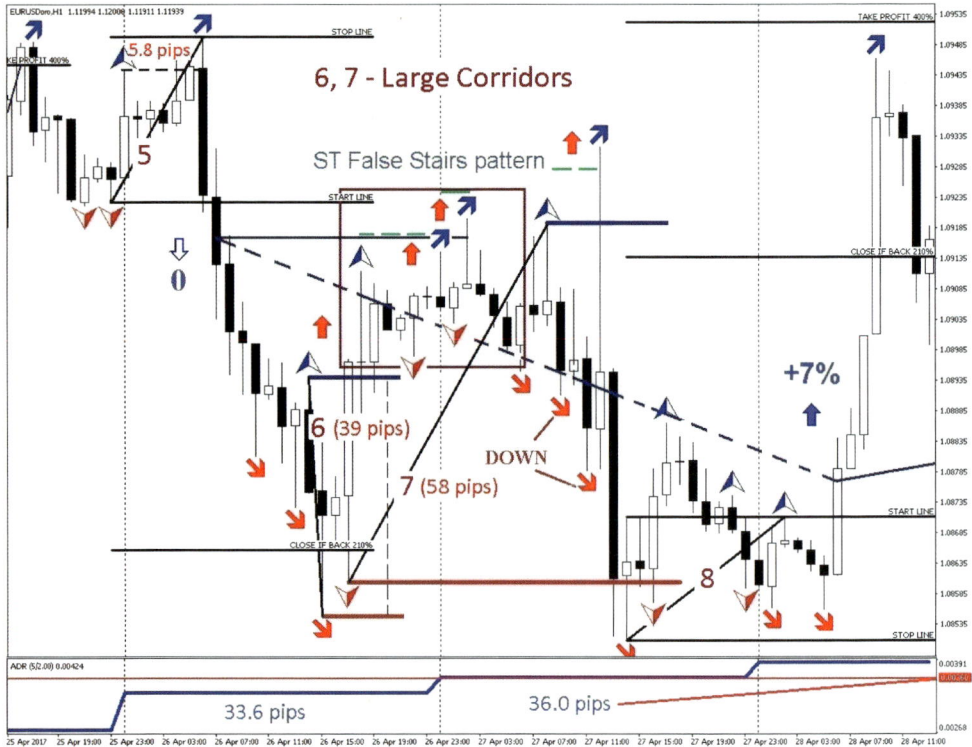

Figure 22: April 26-28

The April 26 trading day began with a false price movement up. It only exceeded the fractal level by 5.8 pips. Thus, prices rushed down through the opposing fractal level with the formation of Corridor № 5, and the ST False Movement Pattern was formed.

The previous movement was upward on the 25th of April, and, therefore, a reversal in price took place. However, in the reversal zone, there is no fully formed opposite fractal. Also, in the reversal zone there is no fractal that is equal or higher than the peak between the broken fractal and the place of the breakdown itself. In this case, the Stop Line must coincide with the high peak between the broken fractal and the intersection point of the Start Line.

Breaking the fractal downward, the price crosses the level of 210%, and then it turns upward, forming Corridor № 6. During the turnout of the previous movement, the Stop Line of Corridor № 6 is placed at the level of the fully formed opposite fractal. The height of this Corridor is 39 pips. Half of the value of the ADR indicator (5) for April 26 is 33.6 pips (including the shortened trading hours of the previous Sunday, April 23). Thus, Corridor № 6 turned out to be Large and does not participate in the game.

On April 27, the price completes the ST False Stairs Pattern, and then, again, breaks the fractal level upward. Corridor № 7 is being formed. The level for its Stop Line is at the level of the fractal that was formed on April 26. The height of Corridor № 7 is 58 pips. Half of the ADR (5) is 36 pips; that is, this Corridor is too large and should not be taken into account.

Without getting support, prices fall down the next day and then build a working Corridor for an upward movement.

April 28: When the price rolls back after a breakthrough upward, the delayed Buy Limit Order (1.08781) is triggered. The Stop Line of Corridor № 8 is placed at the level of the fully formed fractal that appeared on April 27, as its level is lower than the low point between the fractured fractal and the intersection point. The Stop Loss Order is placed at the Stop Line level (1.08508). The counter movement with Corridor № 8 at the base quickly overcomes the level of 210% of its height.

The result of the open transaction will be fixed on May 2 and recorded in the total profit for May. A little before reaching the Stop Line of Corridor № 5 and the Target of 400% from the height of Corridor № 8, the price starts to decrease. The next section of the graph is shown in detail in Figure 23.

Figure 23: EUR/USD for the period from April 28 to May 3, 2017

May 1 is a holiday in many countries. Thus, there is low liquidity in the market. We have an open position on April 28 and a Stop Loss Order set to breakeven level at the moment of reaching the price of 210%. The ST False Stairs Pattern is formed in this market with low liquidity.

May 2: There is a breakthrough of Corridor № 11 downward. The position opened on April 28 closes at the level of 1.08972 with a result of + 7% of the trading account amount. At the same price, the Sell Limit order opens, which, after the appearance of the ST Reverse Movement Pattern, brings a loss of - 10%.

May 3: The ST Direct Movement Pattern, shown in Figure 24, completes the formation of the ST Counter Movement with Direct Movement Pattern, which was shown in Figure 21.

Figure 24: May 3-4

May 3: At the price level of the Start Line of Corridor № 12 minus 6 pips, the Sell Limit Order (1.09183) was triggered. Simultaneously with the opening of the position, the Stop Loss Order was set (1.09375) one pip above the level of the Stop Line of Corridor № 12. The Take Profit Order was set at 1.08745. At 18:00 GMT a decision on the Fed's interest rate was published. No surprises were expected from the release of this data. Immediately after publication, the price dropped to the level of 1.09021, and then reached the Start Line level of Corridor № 12. The level of 210% was at 1.08987.

Accordingly, the level of the turn was not reached, and the Stop Loss Order did not move to break even. Otherwise, the position could be closed prematurely. On the minute chart, shown in Figure 25, this situation is clearly visible.

Figure 25: The jump in prices after the Fed's decision on the interest rate

May 4: After the start of a new trading day, the price tried to reverse in the opposite direction and created the ST False Stairs Pattern. Then, at the level of 400% plus 1 pip, the Take Profit Order was triggered, which brings +21% of the game amount.

The following EUR/USD chart for the period from May 4 to May 11, 2017 is shown in Figure 26.

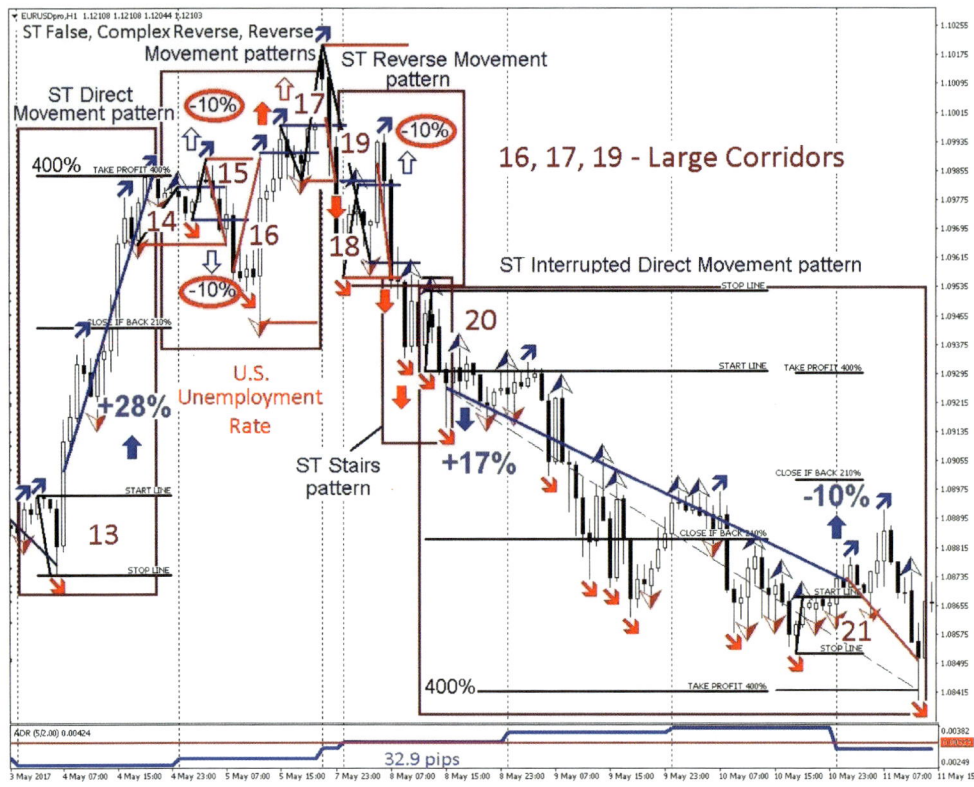

Figure 26: EUR/USD for the period from May 4 to May 11, 2017

May 4: After the breakdown of the Start Line (1.08960) of Corridor № 13 by 7 pips, the Buy Limit Order (1.09030) was triggered. The previous ST Direct Pattern was pointing down, and there was no fully formed downward fractal in the reversal zone lower than the lowest point between the fractured fractal and the intersection point of the Start Line.

In this case, according to the rules, the Stop Line should be set to the low point level that is located between the broken fractal and the intersection point. In this case, the Stop Line is located at the level of not fully formed fractal that appeared before the breakdown. The Stop Loss Order is set to the Stop Line level (1.08739), and the Take Profit Order is set to the level of 400% (1.09840). During the day, the ST Direct Movement Pattern reaches the Target with a result of + 28%. When such fast models appear, the price rollbacks after the breakdown are often minimal. On the EUR/USD minute chart shown in Figure 27, the breakdown area is visible.

Figure 27: May 4, EUR/USD, M1

In this situation, a slight price rollback after the breakdown allowed the Buy Limit Order to be opened at the level of 1.09030. The 10-second chart in the upper left corner shows that after the breakout of the fractal level, the price rolled back to 1.09008. You can review history of seconds and tick quotes yourself by visiting the site: https://tickstory.com.

The period of uncertainty that arose from May 5-8 in connection with the release of the US labor market survey is shown in detail in Figure 28.

30

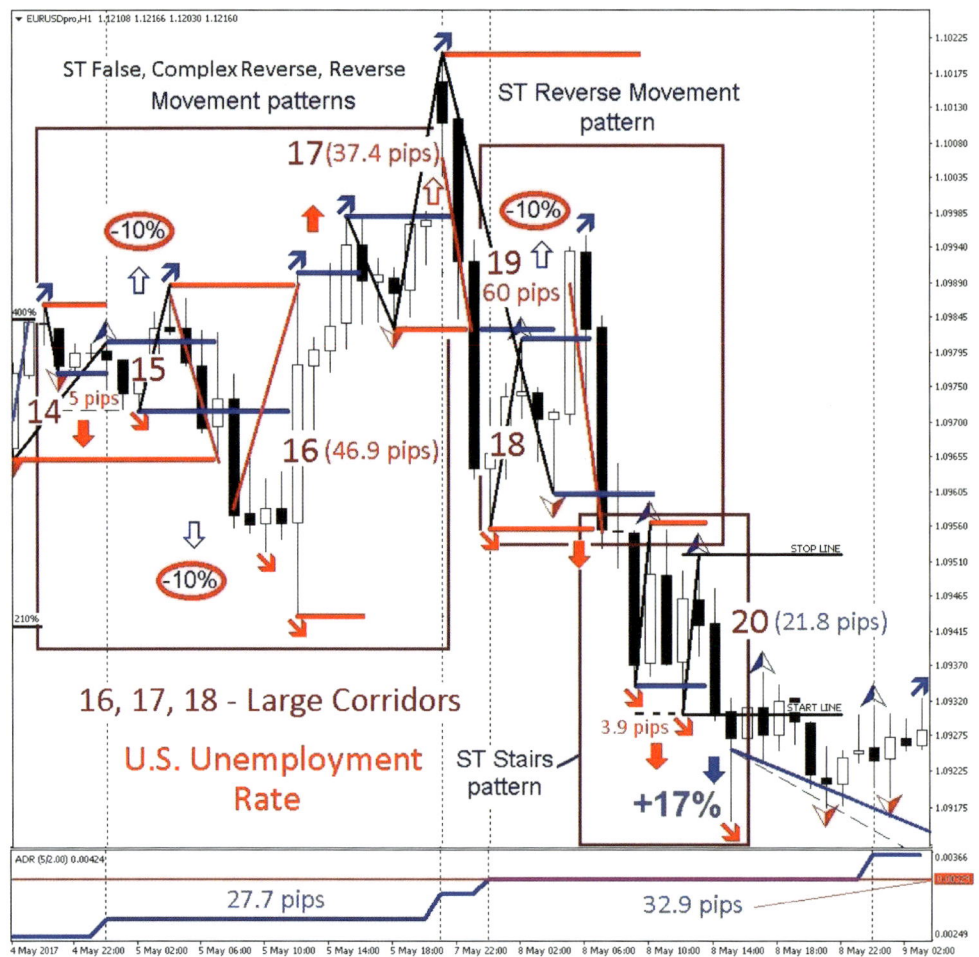

Figure 28: EUR/USD between May 5 and May 8, 2017

May 5: At 12:00, the Employment Situation Summary was expected to be published. For many years these indicators have been considered crucial for decision-making regarding changing interest rates in the United States. In the *Trading Code is Open* book, I explained that the major players leave the market on the eve of the release of this important data.

Publishing values that are different from forecasts can push prices in any direction and even create gaps. Often, before and after the release of this data, a low liquidity market jolts up and down until it settles. In such periods, there is no sense to risk opening deals. It is necessary to wait, when volatility becomes normal and the market, having chosen a direction of movement, starts to draw habitual ST Patterns.

In view of the foregoing, the possible losses that this period of uncertainty can bring will not be taken into account in calculating the overall result for the month. Formed at the end of the trading day by Corridors № 14, № 15, and № 16, the ST False, Complex Reverse, Reverse Movement Pattern clearly demonstrates a period of uncertainty on the chart.

May 8: The next trading week began with a breakdown down of the Large Corridor № 17. Its fractal height was 37.4 pips, and half of the ADR (5) value was 32.9 pips. Abandoned for a time by major players, the market continued to be in uncertainty and high volatility. After the Employment Situation Summary, traders were waiting for the planned comments from FOMC members about the prospects for raising the discount rate. Also, the results of the presidential election held on Sunday, May 7 were discussed.

In this situation, you should not hurry to enter the game immediately after the appearance of the next Corridor, № 18. The desire not to miss a profitable deal in this situation will lead to a loss. The formed ST Reverse Movement Pattern confirmed this by a possible loss of 10% of the deposit. The downward Corridor № 19 was again too large to enter the game. It is necessary to wait until the market consolidates and becomes ready to practice ST Patterns in the usual rhythm.

The minimum technical condition for starting trading after a period of uncertainty can be the emergence of two consecutive Corridors with an allowable fractal height or an apparent consolidation of prices, which is shown in Figure 29.

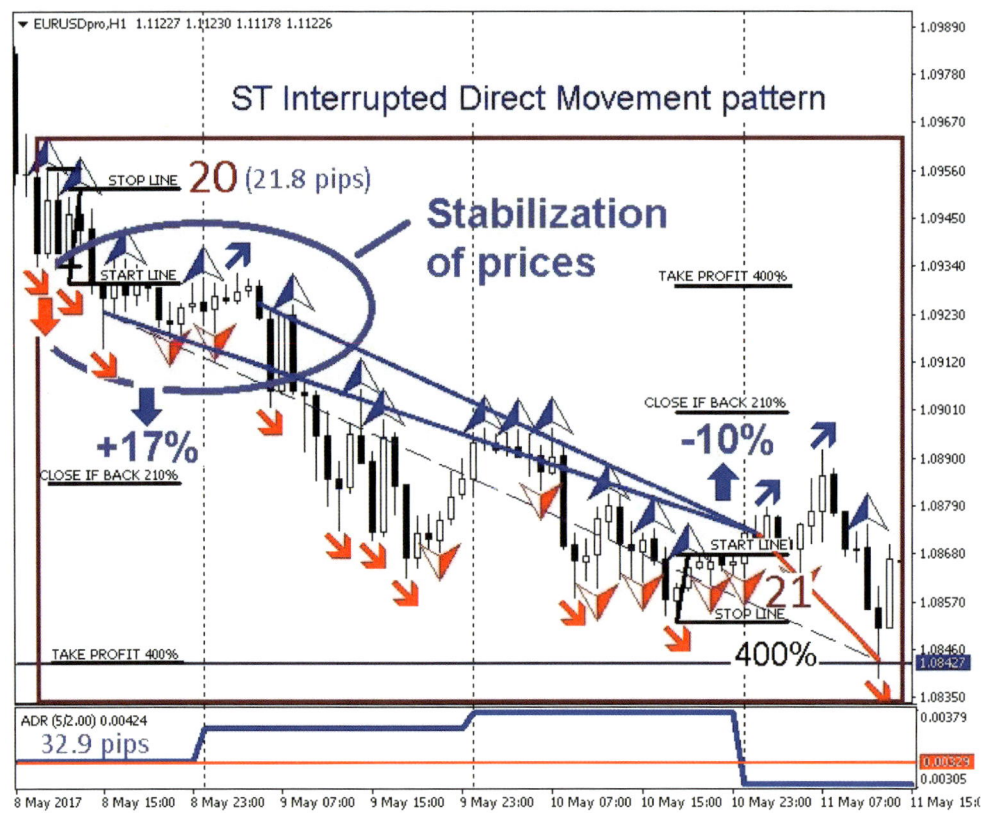

Figure 29: Consolidation of prices

At the end of the working day on May 8, all the expected comments were announced, and the market, creating the Starting ST Stairs Pattern, moved in the downward direction. The Sell Limit Order = 1.09242, the Stop Loss Order = 1.09530, and the Target = 1.08438. The sale could be done immediately after the breakthrough of Corridor № 20 or the next day, after the period of consolidation of prices.

May 9: The price exceeded the level of 210%, and the Stop Loss Order was moved to the breakeven level.

May 10: At the end of the day and a little before reaching the goal, the prices formed Corridor № 21.

May 11: The position closed at the level of 1.08748 with the result + 17% with the break of

Corridor № 21 upward. Simultaneously open at this level, the Buy Limit Order brought a loss of -10%. In the middle of the day, the ST Interrupted Direct Movement Pattern was completed, reaching 400% of the height of Corridor № 20.

The next period, from May 11-16, is shown in Figure 30.

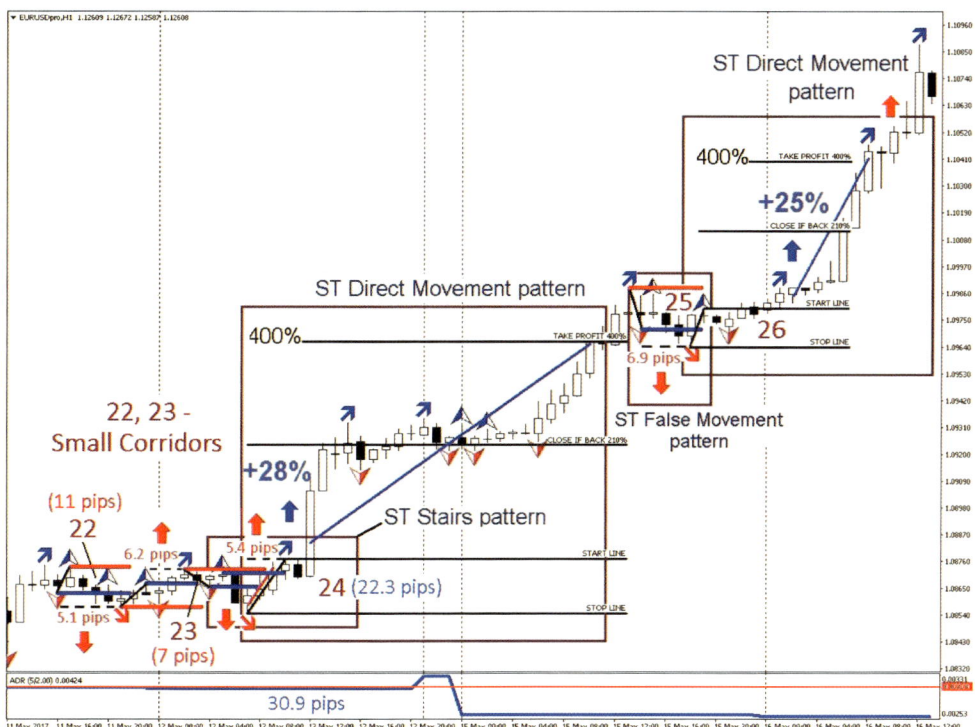

Figure 30: EUR/USD for the period from May 11-16, 2017

May 11: Close to the end of the trading day, a Small Corridor, № 22, appears with a height of 11 pips, which should be skipped.

May 12: Another Small Corridor, № 23, appeared with a height of 7 pips. Then, the price created the ST Stairs Pattern, which became the Starting Line for the ST Direct Movement Pattern. The moment the price returned to the level of the Start Line after its breakdown is shown on the 5-minute chart in Figure 31.

Figure 31: May 12, price return after the breakdown

The rollback of the price after the breakthrough of the fractal level allows you to open the Buy Limit Order at the level of 1.08840. The Stop Loss Order = 1.08547, and the Take Profit Order = 1.09661.

May 15: The ST Direct Movement Pattern with Corridor № 24 at the base, without reverse movements, reached the Target level of 400% and brought + 28%. At the end of the day, Corridor № 25 was formed. The level of the Start Line was overcome by only 6.9 pips.

May 16: Another fast ST Direct Movement Pattern with Corridor № 26 reached the Target. The Buy Limit Order, opened at 1.09959, brought + 25% over a few hours. The Stop Loss Order was set at 1.09755, and the Take Profit Order was set at the level of 1.10587.

The next ST Counter Movement with Direct Movement Pattern, formed between May 16 and 19 is shown in Figure 32.

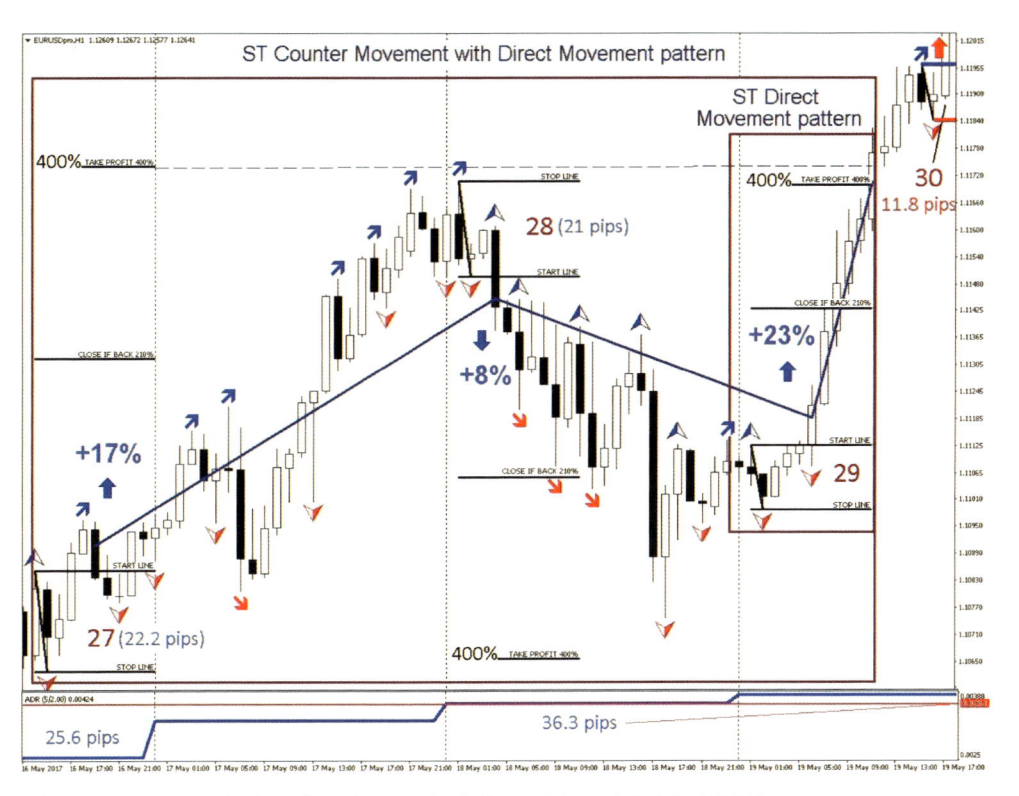

Figure 32: EUR/USD for the period from May 16-19, 2017

May 16: The movement continued upward. After the breakthrough of Corridor № 27, the Buy Limit Order set at 1.10922 was triggered. The Stop Loss Order = 1.10630, and the Take Profit Order = 1.11740.

May 17: Below the level of 210% (1.11318), the price breaks the fractal downward. Under the terms of the strategy, we skipped this movement. Then, the movement went up, and by the end of the day the market was approaching the Target level within 5 pips.

May 18: missing the Target by 3 pips, the price breaks the fractal downward. The initial position closes at the level of 1.11438 with the result of + 17% and at the same level of the Start Line of Corridor № 28 minus 6 pips, the Sell Limit Order is triggered. Stop Loss = 1.11718, Take Profit = 1.10668.

May 19: Below the level of 210% of the height of Corridor № 28, a breakthrough of the upward fractal took place. The position down was closed at 1.11198 and brought + 8%. The Buy Limit Order opened at 1.11198 (Stop Loss = 1.10985, Take Profit = 1.11699), and after a few hours, it reached the Target with a + 23% result. Closer to the end of the trading day, a Small Corridor № 30 with a height of 11.8 pips was formed.

36

The moment of the price rollback after the breakthrough of Fractal Corridor № 29 is shown on the 5-minute chart in Figure 33.

Figure 33: Breakthrough of Corridor № 29

As you can see on the chart, after the breakthrough of the Start Line, the price retreated to the level of 1.11179. This level is below the Buy Limit Order by 1.9 pips.

The formation of the ST Double Complex Reverse Movement Pattern in the period from May 22-30 is shown in Figure 34.

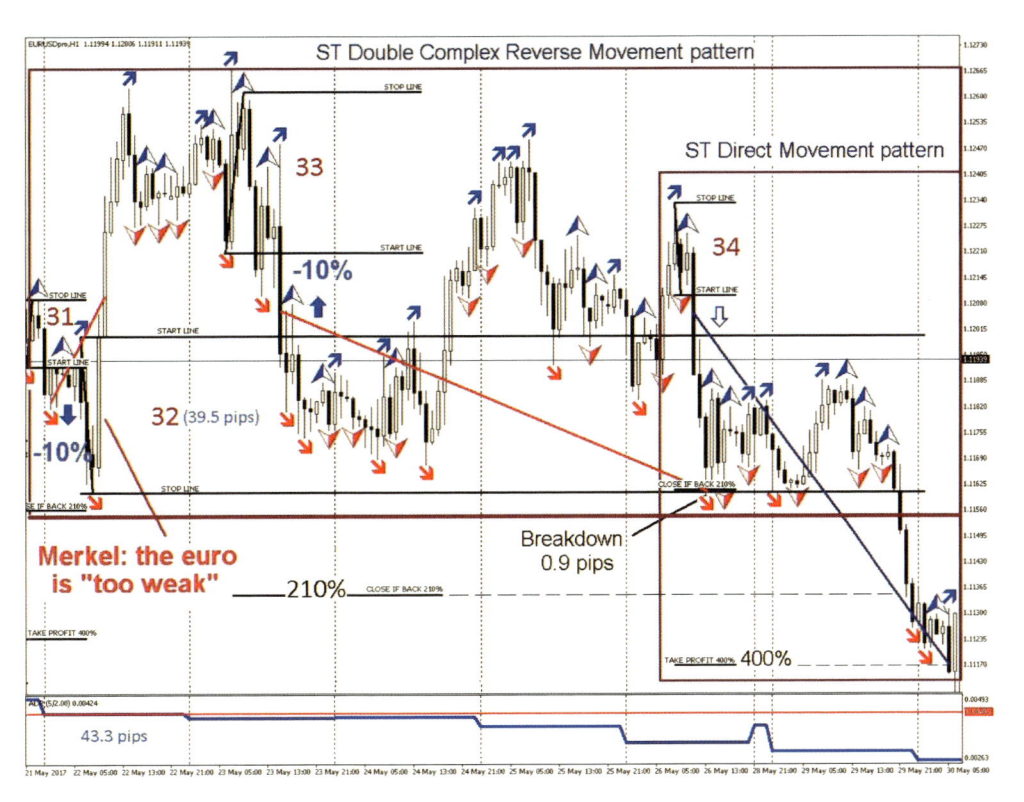

Figure 34: EUR/USD between May 22 and May 30, 2017

May 22: The new trading week began with a breakthrough down the Start Line of Corridor № 31. The downward position had not yet reached the level of 210% of the height of Corridor № 31, as the German Chancellor Merkel said that the euro was "too weak". The market reaction was immediate, and the euro quickly rose to new heights. The Stop Loss Order closed the position with a result of -10%.

May 23: Punctured Corridor № 32 together with Corridor № 31 created the ST Complex Reverse Movement Pattern. The Buy Limit Order was opened at the level of the Start Line of Corridor № 32 plus 7 pips.

May 24, 25, and 26: After verbal intervention, the market unsuccessfully tried to grow during this whole trading week, but it could not reach even the level of 210% of the height of Corridor № 32. On Friday, on the eve of a long weekend in the US and UK, players began to close their positions. On May 26, the Stop Loss Order triggered with a loss of 10%. At that moment, the ST Double Complex Reverse Movement Pattern was formed.

May 29: The price was not able to return to the level of the Start Line of Corridor № 34. After making an attempt to break the fractal upward, the ST

Direct Movement Pattern with Corridor № 34 independently reached the Target of 400%.

The ST Direct Movement Pattern that formed in the last two days of May is shown in Figure 35.

Figure 35: EUR/USD for the period from May 30-31, 2017

May 30-31: The price broke through Corridor № 35. At level 1.1138, the Buy Limit Order was triggered. The Stop Line coincided with the Stop Loss Order and passed through level 1.11087. In the reversal zone, there was no fully formed opposite fractal; therefore, it was determined to set the Stop Line at the low point level between the broken fractal and the intersection point of the Start Line.

After passing the level of 210%, the price overcame the fractal down only by 4.8 pips, which was not enough for a breakthrough. The model was completed when the classic ST Direct Movement Pattern reached the Target of 1.12202 with a result of + 28%.

Let's calculate the total result for the month. Firstly, assume that the amount of the initial account was 1000 conventional units. To this 1000, we should consistently add or subtract all the results obtained in percentages. 1000 + 7%

-10% + 21% + 28% + 17% -10% + 28% + 25% + 17% + 8% + 23% -10% - 10% + 28% = 4049. Thus, the ST Pattern Strategy showed a result equal to approximately 300% of the initial amount for the month.

Surprisingly, this result is equal to the Target profit of ST Patterns Strategy.

Analysis of the GBP/USD Currency Pair

The achievement of real indicators on the stock exchange also depends on other factors. Many of them are described in my first book, *Trading Code is Open*. In this manual, I would like to expand on the impact that uncertainty periods in the market have on trading results. In May, the GBP/USD pair demonstrated a clear example of a period of uncertainty.

The strength of the movement of quotes after a breakthrough is determined by the liquidity of the trading instrument and by the presence of large speculative capital. In times of political or economic uncertainty, the driving force is weakened and becomes inadequate to achieve the Target or Take Profit Order. In such periods, you should leave the trading instrument until the situation becomes clear.

The GBP/USD currency pair has its own character of behavior. The graph is more volatile and creates sweeping cross movements. Often, there are ST Two Counter or ST Three Counter Movement Patterns. This pair also likes to hunt for traders' Stop Loss Orders and crosses the Stop Line for 1-2 pips before continuing the initial move. After the breakout, the price often goes back to the trading Corridor.

These behavioral features require another set of variable values to be used in the trading strategy. Therefore, we take the variable x (breakthrough) equal to 13 pips. The Buy Limit Order is placed at the level of the Start Line plus 4 pips, with the Stop Loss Order set at the Stop Line level minus 2 pips. The Sell Limit Order is set to the Start Line level minus 3 pips, with the Stop Loss Order at the Stop Line level plus 3 pips. Other parameters of the strategy remain the same as those that were used for the EUR/USD pair.

The main objective of the analysis of the GBP/USD pair is to show unfavorable periods in the market. Therefore, we will not go deeply into the daily detailed analysis of the chart until the moment when it is necessary to leave this trading instrument. If desired, you can independently check the results shown below and analyze the ST Patterns. Figures 36 and 37 shows a graph of the GBP/USD currency pair between April 28 and May 17, 2017.

Figure 36: GBP/USD chart for the period from April 28 to May 4, 2017

The rules for forming the ST Zero Pattern were shown in the first book. In this situation, two consecutive identical patterns, formed within three days, did not work. The changing of the Stop Loss Order to the breakeven level after reaching the price level of 210% did not give a +28%. In general, this method, for a long period of time, showed small positive results. If the trader decides to remove the transfer of the Stop Loss Order to the level without loss from his strategy, the trade results will not change significantly.

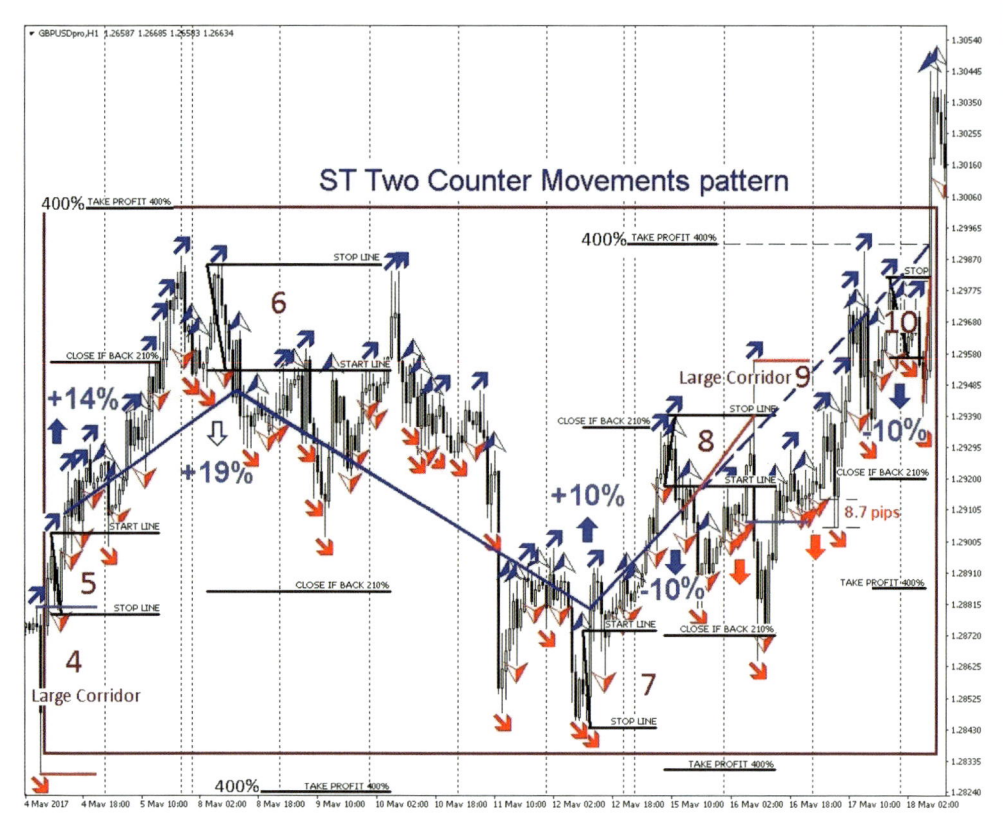

Figure 37: GBP/USD chart for the period from May 4-17, 2017

Over the next almost eleven days, a long ST Two Counter Movement Pattern was formed. In its structure it is similar to the ST Three Counter Movement Pattern that was shown in the first book. The difference between these models is only in the number of opposing movements that overcome the Stop Line of the previous Corridor.

The beginning of the unfavorable period for the GBP/USD pair begins on the chart shown in Figure 38.

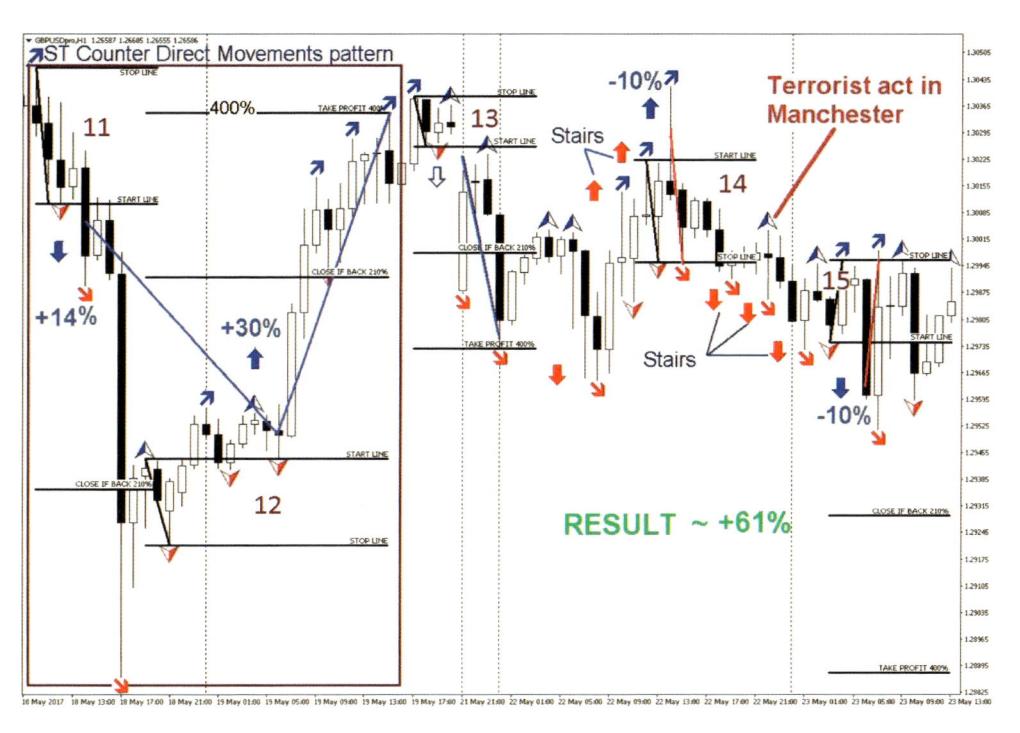

Figure 38: GBP/USD pair from May 18 to May 23

May 18-19: The week ended with a profitable ST Counter Direct Movement Pattern.

May 22: After the appearance of the beginning of the ST Stairs Pattern, there was an opportunity to open a Buy Limit Order at 1.30292. By this time, the result for three weeks was + 79%. During the evening of this day, reports of a terrorist act in Britain began to arrive. The highest level of terrorist threat—"Critical"—was declared.

May 23: The open position to the top was closed after the Stop Loss Order was triggered at 1.29852. After that, it was necessary to finish further trading with the remaining profit of 61%. The unfavorable period in the market is shown in Figures 39 and 40.

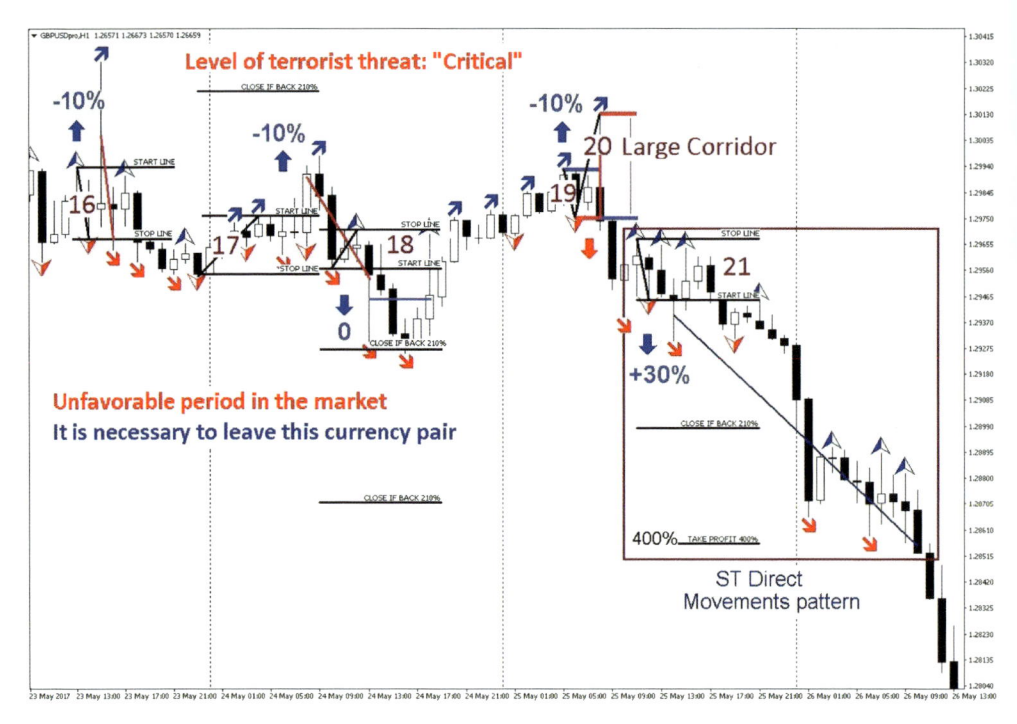

Figure 39: GBP/USD pair from May 23 to May 26

In the next period of time, the GBP/USD currency pair was losing focus and created several ST Complex Reverse Patterns, that were capable of causing a loss of 10% five times. At the end of the week, there were massive sales of the Pound, which formed the ST Direct Movement Pattern. The unfavorable situation was complicated by the upcoming parliamentary elections in the UK scheduled for June 8, 2017.

The period of high volatility is shown in Figure 40.

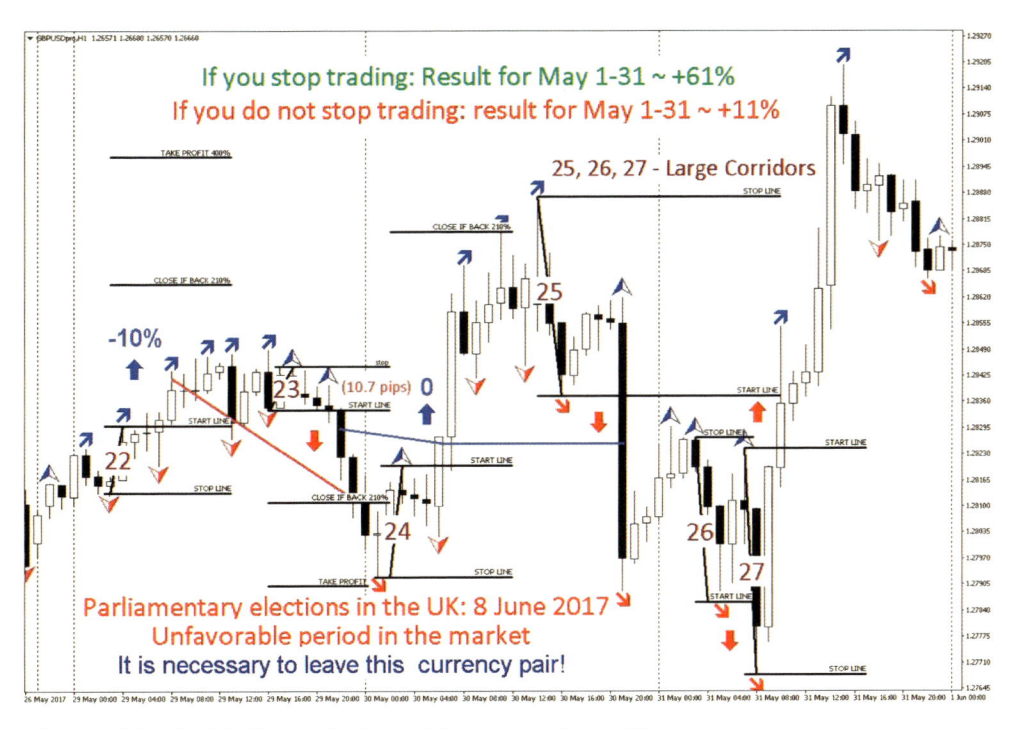

Figure 40: GBP/USD pair from May 29 to May 31

The GBP/USD pair, abandoned by large players, demonstrated high volatility, which, as a rule, confirms unfavorable periods. Continuing to trade in such a low liquidity market, you can lose a substantial part of your deposit. In this case, continuing to trade in an unfavorable period would have left the trader with only 11% of the profit. However, continuing to trade until June 8 could have made the result even worse.

The results of the ST Patterns Strategy published in the book Trading Code is Open were obtained based on historical data without taking into account many unfavorable periods in the market. Therefore, sometimes there are months with a minimum and even a negative yield in the calculations. For example, the unfavorable period in the market was after Brexit and the presidential elections in the US.

Decisions about interest rate changes by central banks strongly influence the behavior of the market. At the same time, the US Fed is trying to pursue a more predictable financial policy than, for example, the monetary authorities of the European Union. Military conflicts and their exacerbations also play an important role in market activity.

Understanding the importance of stopping trade during unfavorable periods in the market has a great impact on the results of trading. The trader should closely monitor economic and political events. The dispute between technical and fundamental analysts for day trading is decided in favor of the former. When there is a significant fundamental event, it is better to wait outside the market.

EUR/USD, M5

All examples of the strategy's work were shown on hourly charts as an optimal timeframe variant. Using smaller time periods, it's also possible to get excellent results. However, different brokers sometimes have different quotes. In small timeframes, these differences can occur more often, and fractal levels may not coincide with the values shown in the examples. To demonstrate the flexibility of the strategy settings and the formation of short-term uncertainty periods, the EUR/USD pair is shown below on five-minute charts in one working day on May 31.

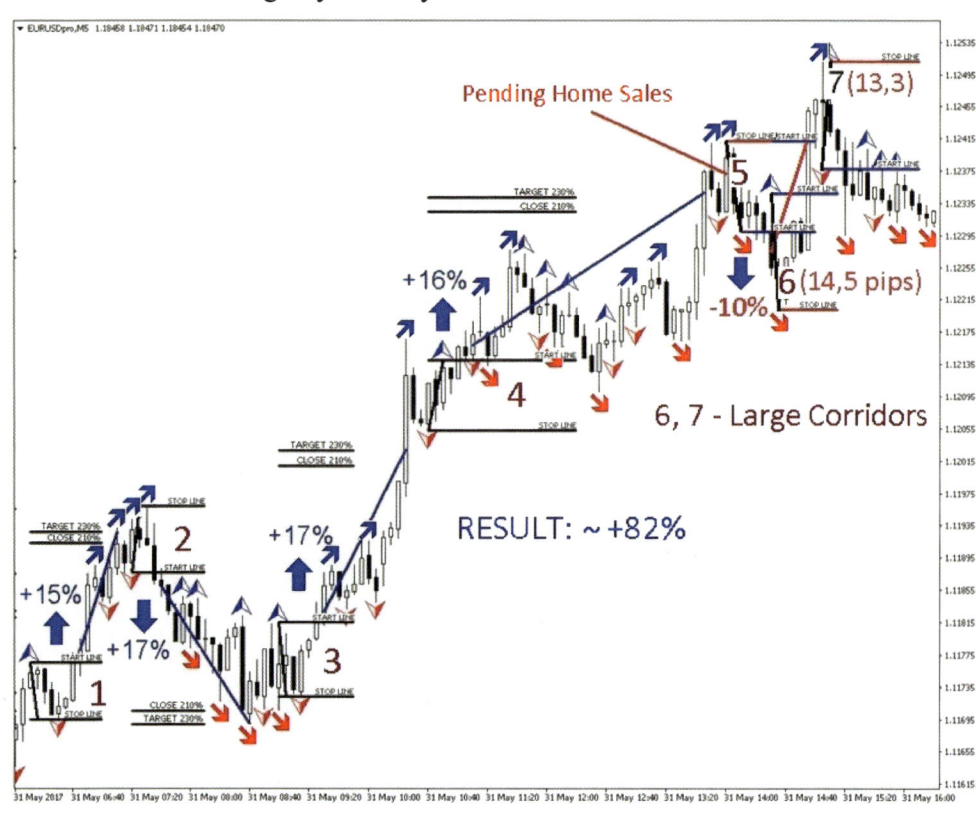

Figure 41: Pair EUR/USD, M5, May 31, 2017

To analyze this graph, the following strategy parameters were applied: Breakthrough = 2.2 pips, Spread = 0.7 pip, Buy Limit Order = Start Line + 2.2 pips, Sell Limit Order = Start Line - 1.5 pip, Stop Loss Order = Stop Line, Target = 230%, Close If Back = 210%, possible loss = - 10% of the deposit. We use all Fractal Corridors with a height of 2.0 pips to 13.0 pips.

To analyze this graph, the following rules were applied for a Long position:

1. Find in history the nearest completed ST Pattern (It's better if it's an ST Direct Movement Pattern).

2. Find the next Fractal Corridor formed by opposite fractals (peak and valley), no smaller than 2 pips and not larger than 12 pips.

3. If № 2 is met: Find the level of breakdown (BDL) X pips above the upper Fractal Corridor level (Start Line). For M5, EUR/USD, $X = 2.2$ pips.

4. If the price reaches the BDL: Buy Order Level is Y pips above the Start Line. The value for $Y=X=2.2$ (or another value depending on tactics and spread). Wait for the price to roll back to push the trigger.

5. Now the position is open. Two things can develop: a) The price turns against the trade and hits the Stop Loss Order Level or b) The price can reach the 210% level (Turn Level).

6. If the price reaches the 210% level, then either: a) The price will continue up to the 230% (or 400%) Target Level or b) The price can turn away, in the opposite direction of our trade.

7. While we are between the 210% and 230% (or 400%) levels: A new position is opened downward if any Fractal Corridor is punched down by the value = X. At the same time, the starting position is closed.

The deal closes when the price reaches the Target Level of 230% (or 400%) of the height of the initial Fractal Corridor.

8. The same rules apply for a Short position.

The graph shows how starting from 6:00 GMT, Corridor №s 1, 2, 3, 4 consistently form four ST Direct Movement Patterns. For nine hours of work, the result was approximately + 82% of the initial deposit. At 14:00 GMT, the economic output of Pending Home Sales (MoM) (Apr) was planned. This event is significant, and at the time of publication of these data, there is a possibility of high volatility in the market.

The degree of importance of data is reflected in economic calendars, which are published by many financial sites, for instance, www.investing.com/economic-calendar/. At the time of important events, it is better to stay out of the market.

The previous value of Pending Home Sales = - 0.9%, the forecast = + 0.5%, and the value = - 1.3%. The data is significantly different from the forecast, and the market forms an ST Reverse Pattern and two Fractal Corridors that are too Large. A short period of uncertainty is formed. In this situation, you should wait until the market calms down, volatility becomes normal, and a new ST Pattern is formed. After that, the work could be continued if you carefully follow the news.

It should be noted that, in contrast to working on hourly charts for short-term trading, greater reaction speed and maximum concentration of attention is required. The potential for possible profit also increases in such situation.

Conclusion

You can lose many years studying well-known, but useless, trading strategies. Many financial corporations and brokers spend millions of dollars on advertising and promoting non-working trading systems, suggesting their high profitability. For them, it's just a way to attract new customers, most of whom will soon lose their deposits.

Personally, over the past 18 years, I have not learned any trading strategy that could show the carefully verified results presented here. As a rule, trading strategies that appear to be as successful at first sight, cannot withstand careful testing. As the saying goes, "the truth is in the details." Success on the exchange markets, perhaps like anywhere else, consists of many small things.

Most traders have spent years looking for a method of technical analysis that is able to generate profits. In order to popularize the ST Patterns Strategy, the author welcomes the creation of an ST Patterns thread of discussion on Forex forums and other platforms for traders to discuss trading strategies, as long as the original name and source are preserved.

In conclusion, I would like to recall once again that a working technical system is a necessary, but not sufficient, condition for obtaining real results. Emotion and discipline play an important role in the implementation of the trading system. In turn, automatic trading systems are not able to take into account all the nuances necessary for playing on the exchanges.

The trader should closely monitor changes in the market and make timely adjustments to the variable values of his trading system. This applies not only to the magnitude of the breakout, but also to other parameters, such as the distance to the target, the amount of rollback, and other variable parameters.

More details about trading robots and the influence of various factors on the performance of a trader can be found in the book *Trading Code is Open*.

I started writing my first book for traders who have already made their professional choice and are in search of a working technical trading strategy. However, the presented results can give hope to those who are not yet familiar with the harsh laws of the exchange.

To those newcomers who are counting on easy success, I must warn you: not many are able to successfully and permanently work on the exchange. High profits only exist due to the fact that the vast majority of players lose. Honestly answer this question for yourself: are you really a universal soldier? And do not believe those who say that making money on the exchange is easy!

P. S.

Dear traders! The third book, *Trading Strategy: Fractal Corridors on the Futures, CFD and Forex Markets*, continues the publication of the ST Patterns Strategy.

To simplify the construction of models, the rules for working with the four basic ST Patterns, which are common for all graphic combinations, have been emphasized. The rule of excluding completed Corridors from the game can facilitate the analysis of complex models.

A detailed technical analysis of the EUR/USD chart for the period from July 1 to August 31, 2017 shows a result equal to +800% of the initial deposit. The influence of economic news coming out on schedule is shown, which, if taken into account, has the potential to significantly increase the received profit.

Contact

Send your questions, wishes, and suggestions through the feedback form on the website https://stpatterns.com.

Printed in Great Britain
by Amazon